I pray that from God's glorious, unlimited resources God will empower you with inner strength through The Spirit.

Then Christ will make his home in your hearts as you trust in him. Your roots will grow down into God's love and keep you strong.

And may you have the power to understand, as all God's people should, how wide, how long, how high, and how deep God's love is.

May you experience the love of Christ, though it is too great to understand fully.

Then you will be made complete with all the fullness of life and power that comes from God.[1]

Ephesians 3:16-19

---

[1] Harrison, ed., *NLT Study Bible: New Living Translation* (Carol Stream, IL: Tyndale House Publishers, Inc., 2008). [With slight changes by Sue.]

Contemporary Fiction by Susan McGeown:

Recipe for Disaster

Rules for Survival

A Well Behaved Woman's Life

The Butler Did It

Joining The Club

Embracing The Truth

Historical Fiction by Susan McGeown:

A Garden Walled Around Trilogy:
Call Me Bear
Call Me Elle
Call Me Survivor

Rosamund's Bower

No Darkness So Great

Windermere Plantation

Nonfiction by Susan McGeown:

Biblical Women and Who They Hooked Up With

Biblical Warrior Women and Their Weapons

Jerusalem Times:

JT: The Jesus of Nazareth Edition

JT: The Twelve Apostles Edition

God's Phoenix Woman

The Rise of the Mighty (A Study of Acts)

What We Believe (A Study of Romans)

C.S. Lewis & Me

Old Testament 101

The Parables of Jesus

A Book of Thanks

Prayer & Me

A Book of Blessing

A Verse A Day.

Advice on Marriage, Love, and Friendship From Someone Who's Been There

In Case of Fire Take These Books!

Quality Reads for People of Faith

By Susan McGeown

Faith Inspired Books

Published by Faith Inspired Books
3 Kathleen Place, Bridgewater, New Jersey 08807
susanmcgeown@faithinspiredbooks.com
www.FaithInspiredBooks.com
Copyright December, 2024

All Rights Reserved

ISBN: 978-1-946268-14-3

The quoted ideas expressed in this book (but not the scripture verses) are not, in all cases, exact quotations but rather obtained from secondary sources, primarily print media. In every case, the author has made every effort to maintain the speaker's original intent. While every effort was made to ensure the accuracy of these sources, the accuracy cannot be guaranteed. For additions, deletions, corrections, or clarifications please contact Susan McGeown at the above address.

Bibliographic credit appears at the end of this work.

Merry Christmas Precious Sisters and Brothers!

Here we are at the end of another year. Does the time go faster each year for you? (It does for me.)

This year's book is somewhat of a departure from what I usually do. It's kind of like a big advertisement for *other books* you should be reading. I initially struggled with what to put together (usually it hits me early in the year and I gradually put it together as the year passes) but this year, by mid-October I had nothing. I prayed about it, looked in my vast collections of computer notes (and books started but never finished) and found … nothing. And then, I turned around and looked at my "most precious books shelf" (it's immediately behind my desk so that I can reach up and grab one whenever I need it) and I chuckled to myself and thought, "If there was ever a fire, I'd have to grab these books!" and BAM, I had my book idea.

I've struggled with a lot of things this year – personally, politically, and spiritually. In many ways it has been a year more difficult than the worst pandemic year was. But through it all, your prayers, support, and encouragement have been the bright and shining light that have kept me moving forward. I read recently[2] that light is not something to be looked at, but rather the medium in which all other things are visible. Jesus called himself the light of the world (Jn. 8:12), but do you realize he called *us* to be the light, too (Matt. 5:14)? When I read that, I thought of many of you who have spoken with me directly (through my tears sometimes), or texted me encouraging words knowing I was struggling, or prayed faithfully for me … and in doing so were the light I needed to keep seeing.

---

[2] My newest read is currently Richard Rohr's *The Universal Christ* Richard Rohr, *The Universal Christ* (New York: Covergent Books, n.d.).

Love you all so very much.

I don't know where I would be without you, but it would not be a place any more blessed than this.

Love,

Sue

Zephaniah 3:17

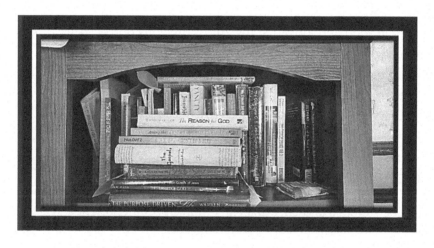

My "In Case of Fire" Bookshelf...

Table of Contents

My Thoughts

First and foremost, I am a believer in Jesus Christ; his life, death and resurrection. I believe that He was God on earth with us and that the example he set and that is recorded in our Gospels (Matthew, Mark, Luke, and John) are The Best Sources for understanding God and what God wants from us lowly humans.

That being said, I also will be the first person to acknowledge that there is not one religion (or individual for that matter) that has completely and accurately described or fully revealed Who God Truly Is. This is the goal every human being on the planet should be working on: to know and understand God better than is currently known. With an open attitude like that, we should prayerfully and carefully continue to ask questions, acknowledge our doubts and confusions, and search for answers and insights ... *forever.* At least until we're in the box...

I have come to believe that doubts and questions are God's gifts to us. They are the windows that God is inviting us to peer into (and perhaps even climb through) to know God better. (By the way, if you have no questions or doubts, then you've made your God tiny, I'm sorry to tell you.) With the Spirit's presence within us guiding us, we can continue to grow and learn and transform so that we eventually become unrecognizable from our original selves! YIPPEE!!

Scripture, primarily the Gospels, is the best way to understand – through the life, teachings, death and resurrection of Jesus Christ – what God desires for creation. Humanity, God's crowning achievement of creation, is called to be God's reflection here on earth: the salt and light to the darkness this world is enduring.

Besides studying Scripture, I have been blessed with "standing on the shoulders" of those believers that have gone before me. It is a privilege to be able to discover what God has revealed to others in ways that best suit their circumstances, abilities, and needs. Seminary has helped me discover a vast library of sources that I have only begun to examine. The books mentioned in this book are ones that *so far* have been essential in my spiritual journey. They have challenged me, changed me, corrected me, and blessed me. They are listed here in no particular ranking, but I have separated them into "Daily Devotionals" and "Books to Read" just for clarity.

Just like creation, the diversity within these writings encompasses all areas: topics, styles of writing, depths of writing, differences in formats... Some you may like and some you may not. (Some will probably make you realize just how very different we are.[3]) *That's a good thing. That's how God designed us.* The diversity we see and feel in this world is a reflection of the vastness of our God that is too inscrutable for human minds to understand.

I'm one of those readers that loves to have the print book in my hand. I write and underline and comment and draw emojis... no one wants my copy when I'm done. When I buy gift copies for others of a particular book, I list those individuals in the back of my copy. When I have questions or find insight for something else I may need in the future, I make note of key page numbers in the front cover. I fold over corners, stick in post-it notes, too. (See, I knew you wouldn't want to read my copy!) BUT, if a book is *really, really good* I also invest in a Kindle e-copy that I can have with me wherever I go on my Kindle phone app. All of these books are of that status. Oh, and I always buy used if possible. Save the planet!

Much of these precious authors/books have resulted from reading *other* precious authors/books. Make note of that. If you read

---

[3] "Ewww, this book was *awful*. What was Sue thinking?!" LOL

a quote that "hits you between the eyes," check that individual out! Footnotes – those often-overlooked blurbs at the bottom of your pages – often are the conversations the author wishes to have with *you*, the reader. I regularly find all sorts of interesting things there; you should always make the effort to read them – at least in the beginning to get a feel for how the author "uses" them.

If you find an author you like or are curious about, and they are prolific in their writing, try finding a compendium or "greatest hits" work. (These are often packaged as devotionals.) This is a great way to get a cross section of an author and also find additional works that are worth reading in more depth.

It is my earnest prayer that you will receive some of the insight and blessings that I have received from reading these books. I look forward – in a few years – to writing a "Volume II." Perhaps you will write me and recommend something!

Blessings,

Sue McGeown

Philippians 1:20-21

Romans 15:13

I ponder every morsel of wisdom from you,
I attentively watch how you've done it.
I relish everything you've told me of life,
I won't forget a word of it.[4]
Psalm 119:15-16

DAILY

DEVOTIONALS

---

[4] Eugene H. Peterson, *The Message: The Bible In Contemporary Language* (NavPress, 2006).

DAILY DEVOTIONALS

DAILY DEVOTIONALS

Howard Thurman: Meditations of the Heart[6]

BOOK SNIP

Type:
This is a daily devotional.

Topic Focus:
This is a spiritual smorgasbord of thoughts, prayers, and meditations regarding all aspects of our faith relationship with God.

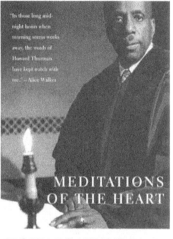

HOWARD THURMAN

Sue's Thoughts;
Howard Thurman was an ordained minister who has the distinction of being the cofounder of the first inter-racially co-pastored church in America (the Church for the Fellowship of All Peoples in San Francisco, CA).[7] He had a "profound" influence on the Rev. Martin Luther King, Jr. in seeing the value of nonviolence.[8]

The first time I encountered Howard Thurman was in seminary, for my "Intro to New Testament" class.[9] We were assigned to read his

---

[5] Howard Thurman, *Meditations of the Heart* (Boston, MA: Beacon Press, 1981), 81.
[6] Thurman, *Meditations of the Heart*.
[7] https://www.fellowshipsf.org/
[8] https://www.smithsonianmag.com/history/this-theologian-helped-mlk-see-value-nonviolence-180967821/
[9] I'm waving to Dr. Virginia Wiles!

book *Jesus and the Disinherited.*[10]   Thurman introduced me to a Jesus I had never known who was a captive, enslaved, oppressed, despised individual who spent most of his life with his "back against the wall."[11] It was such a powerful book that I asked the professor to recommend another one by Thurman that I should read. I remember her looking me directly in the eyes and saying, *"Any one. They're all good."*

Thurman was a prolific writer and so I was a bit overwhelmed when I looked him up. And then I found *Meditations of the Heart.* It's a perfect "first" book to read by him because it is a compilation of many of his works, fed to you in nice, daily bites. The number of times I sat, overwhelmed with insight and blessing, after reading an entry was astounding. My copy is filled with notes in the margins, underlines and corners folded over to gain quick reference. I can't tell you how much it blessed and changed me. As you can imagine, choosing just a few favorite quotes to put in here was very difficult!

Favorite Quote(s):

- "…there is in every person an inward sea, and in that sea there is an island and on that island there is an altar and standing guard before that altar is the "angel with the flaming sword." Nothing can get by that angel to be placed upon that altar unless it has the mark of your inner authority. Nothing passes "the angel with the flaming sword" to be placed upon your altar unless it be a part of "the fluid area of your consent." This is your crucial link with the Eternal."[12]
- "I shall study how so to love myself that, in my attitude toward myself, I shall be pleasing to God and face with confidence what He requires of me."[13]

---

[10] Howard Thurman, *Jesus and the Disinherited* (Boston, MA: Beacon Press, 1976).
[11] Thurman. p. xvi.
[12] Thurman, *Meditations of the Heart,* 5.
[13] Thurman, 47.

DAILY DEVOTIONALS

- "Often, to be free means the ability to deal with the realities of one's situation so as not to be overcome by them."[14]
- What is right in the light of the present set of facts may not be able to stand up under the scrutiny of unfolding days."[15]
- "Again and again, we are reminded by the facts of our own lives that there is an aspect of our experience which seems to be beyond our own control and yet which seems ever to manipulate us into position."[16]
- "Here is the Hand that reaches out to hold and in holding, rescues. Here is the Animated Confidence that undergirds and sustains. In the quietness of this hour, I saturate myself with the spirit of the living God which is THE answer to all the shocks that await me on tomorrow."[17]
- When we have exhausted our store of endurance,
  When our strength has failed ere the day is half done,
  When we reach the end of our hoarded resources,
  Our Father's full giving is only begun."[18]
- "If I knew you and you knew me,
  And each of us could clearly see
  By that inner light divine
  The meaning of your heart and mine:
  I'm sure that we would differ less
  And clasp our hands in friendliness,
  If you knew me, and I knew you."[19]
- "It is a source of immeasurable satisfaction and comfort to me to know that God, who is the Source and Sustainer of life, can be trusted to see me all the way to the end and beyond."[20]

---

[14] Thurman, 54.
[15] Thurman, 80.
[16] Thurman, 93.
[17] Thurman, 97.
[18] Thurman, 110.
[19] Thurman, 116.
[20] Thurman, 125.

DAILY DEVOTIONALS

- "I surrender to God the nerve center of my consent. This is the very core of my will, the mainspring of my desiring, the essence of my conscious thought."[21]

Book Summary[22]:

Meditations of the Heart is a beautiful collection of meditations and prayers by one of our greatest spiritual leaders. Howard Thurman, the great spiritualist and mystic, was renowned for the quiet beauty of his reflections on humanity and our relationship with God. This collection of fifty-four of his most well-known meditations features his thoughts on prayer, community, and the joys and rituals of life. Within this collection are words that sustain, elevate, and inspire. Thurman addresses those moments of trial and uncertainty and offers a message of hope and endurance for people of all faiths.

Purchase Tips:

Always tried to buy used! *Always.*

Author Profile[23]:

Howard Thurman (1900-1981) was the first black dean of Marsh Chapel at Boston University and cofounder of the Church for the Fellowship of All Peoples in San Francisco, California, the first inter-racially co-pastored church in America.

---

[21] Thurman, 163.
[22] All book summaries are cut and pasted from Amazon's website, however each one is the specific book summary put out by each book's publisher.
[23] This profile is the author's official biography available on Amazon.

DAILY DEVOTIONALS

"Transformed people transform people."[24]

Richard Rohr: Yes, And...[25]

BOOK SNIP

Type:
This is a daily devotional.

Topic Focus:
Focusing on all aspects of faith, this book is an excellent compilation of many of Fr. Rohr's many writings and podcasts. It focuses on saying, "Yes" to God ... and then what comes next.

Sue's Thoughts;
Fr. Richard Rohr writes, speaks, and does podcasts. His ministry, Center for Action and Contemplation,[26] spans denominationally and globally. This book, *Yes, And...* is a compilation of many of these mediums and is an excellent source to guide you towards which of his books you will read next (which you most definitely will want to do!).

Seminary has taught me to look and listen and learn from denominations and faiths other than my usuals (Baptist/Reformed/Protestant). Although a believer from an early age, my circle of influence (and hence belief) has been very small. When you add in my preference towards introverted and solitary pursuits...well, you

---

[24] Richard Rohr, *Yes, And...* (Cincinnati, OH: Franciscan Media, 1997), 55.
[25] Rohr, *Yes, And...*
[26] www.cac.org

can just guess the result. No one faith is perfect when attempting to understand God and we must remember that all goodness comes from God – not just the thoughts with which we are familiar.

I can't remember how I found Fr. Rohr. I've taken, in my reading, to make note of quotes other authors referenced from other individuals. As Fr. Rohr is often quoted, I suspect that's how we first encountered each other. The fact that he is a Catholic priest (a Franciscan) was a new venture for me. But, just like me, he seems to "get in trouble" sometimes with the "authorities above" because he doesn't always "fit the approved mold" of what is considered "acceptable and correct." *(Go, Richard!)*

Fr. Rohr's writings have empowered and encouraged me to be the person God most wants me to be. I would go as far as to say his writing has been some of the greatest influences in my spiritual journey.

Favorite Quote(s):

- "Spirituality is always about how we see. It's not about earning or achieving some kind of merit. Once you see rightly, the rest follows and the road widens."[27]
- "Literalism[28] is the lowest and most narrow hermeneutic[29] for understanding conversation in general and sacred tests in particular."[30]
- "Every viewpoint is a view from a point, and we need to critique our own perspective if we are to see and follow the full truth."[31]
- "Holy people are in one sense profoundly conservative, knowing that they merely stand on the shoulders of their ancestors and will be shoulders to support generations to come. They are only a

[27] Rohr, *Yes, And...*, 195.
[28] "Literalism" is interpreting words in the usual or most basic sense.
[29] "Hermeneutic" is how we interpret the Bible or other texts.
[30] Rohr, *Yes, And...*, 75.
[31] Rohr, 39.

part of the Eternal Mystery of God unfolding in time, *and yet they are a part!* Yet these same people are often quite liberal and reforming because they have no private agendas or self-interest to protect…It is all about God for them, and they are just along for the ride."[32]

- "Scripture clearly says, in many ways, that God helps those who *trust in God*, not those who help themselves."[33]
- "All God appears to want from us is honesty and humility."[34]
- "God is not only stranger than we think, but stranger than the logical mind can think…The belief in God as a Trinity is saying God is more an active verb than a stable noun."[35]
- "Kingdom people feel like grounded yet spacious people at the same time, the best of the conservative and the best of the progressive types in the same body."[36]

Book Summary[37]:

Featuring meditations and prayers for every day of the year, Yes, And… supports the reader on their journey with their Christian faith. It offers a refreshing and open-minded approach to living out your faith. World-renowned spiritual teacher Richard Rohr offers an extensive collection of his thoughts and teachings for the reader to apply to their daily life. This guide supports those on their journey to find spiritual relevance in an open-minded way through excerpts from his many written and recorded works.

This deeply uplifting and all-encompassing book is broken down to seven different spiritual themes that follow.

---

[32] Rohr, 288.

[33] Rohr, 311.

[34] Rohr, 347.

[35] Rohr, 381.

[36] Rohr, 399.

[37] All book summaries are cut and pasted from Amazon's website, however each one is the specific book summary put out by each book's publisher.

21

Methodology: Scripture as validated by experience, and experience as validated by tradition, are good scales for one's spiritual worldview.

Foundation: If God is Trinity and Jesus is the face of God, then it is a benevolent universe. God is not someone to be afraid of but is the Ground of Being and on our side.

Frame: There is only one reality. Any distinction between natural and supernatural, sacred and profane is a bogus one.

Ecumenical: Everything belongs, and no one needs to be scapegoated or excluded. Evil and illusion only need to be named and exposed truthfully, and they die in exposure to the light.

Transformation: The separate self is the problem, whereas most religion and most people make the "shadow self" the problem. This leads to denial, pretending, and projecting instead of real transformation into the Divine.

Process: The path of descent is the path of transformation. Darkness, failure, relapse, death, and woundedness are our primary teachers, rather than ideas or doctrines.

Goal: Reality is paradoxical and complementary. Non-dual thinking is the highest level of consciousness. Divine union, not private perfection, is the goal of all religion.

Purchase Tips:
Always tried to buy used! *Always.*

Author Profile[38]:
Fr. Richard Rohr is a globally recognized ecumenical teacher bearing witness to the universal awakening within Christian mysticism and the Perennial Tradition. He is a Franciscan priest of the New Mexico

---

[38] This profile is the author's official biography available on Amazon.

DAILY DEVOTIONALS

Province and founder of the Center for Action and Contemplation (www.cac.org) in Albuquerque, New Mexico, where he also serves as Academic Dean of the Living School for Action and Contemplation. Fr. Richard's teaching is grounded in the Franciscan alternative orthodoxy--practices of contemplation and self-emptying, expressing itself in radical compassion, particularly for the socially marginalized.

Fr. Richard is author of numerous books, including Everything Belongs, Adam's Return, The Naked Now, Breathing Under Water, Falling Upward, Immortal Diamond, and Eager to Love.

He has been a featured essayist on NPR's "This I Believe," a guest of Mehmet Oz on the Oprah and Friends radio show, and a guest of Oprah Winfrey on Super Soul Sunday. Fr. Richard was one of several spiritual leaders featured in the 2006 documentary film ONE: The Movie and was included in Watkins' Spiritual 100 List for 2013. He has given presentations with spiritual leaders such as Rob Bell, Cynthia Bourgeault, Joan Chittister, Shane Claiborne, James Finley, Laurence Freeman, Thomas Keating, Ronald Rolheiser, Jim Wallis, and the Dalai Lama.

"Keep partnering with Me to work out the change you want to see in your life."[39]

Jennifer LeClaire: Mornings With The Holy Spirit[40]

BOOK SNIP

Type:
This is a daily devotional.

Topic Focus:
The author writes from the perspective of God's still small voice providing a profoundly loving personal dialogue. Scripture suggestions and a prayer is provided for each day.

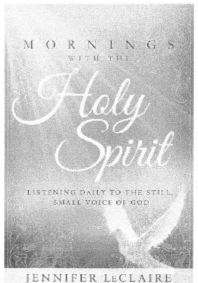

Sue's Thoughts;
I picked up this book at the local Bible book store years ago (my copy is in a journal/devotional format with a pretty turquoise leather cover that I admit I fell for before I even looked inside). I was prepping to do an upcoming women's conference on the Holy Spirit and it seemed to be a little too perfect! I had never heard of the author.

---

[39] Jennifer LeClaire, *Mornings With The Holy Spirit* (Lake Mary, FL: Charisma House, n.d.), 103.
[40] LeClaire, *Mornings With The Holy Spirit*.

DAILY DEVOTIONALS

At first the book put me off because you see the writer composes her entries as if she is God speaking to you. I initially thought that was a bit … Presumptuous? Bold? Over-confident? Insolent? I mean, come on, who thinks they can talk and advise like God? But then I started to read the book… Each day, you are given: Scripture to look up and read, a brief paragraph in which "God" is speaking to you, and a prayer for you to articulate. The insight and encouragement are tremendous.

I read this book not once, but twice from cover to cover. During my reading of this book, I had the singularly, greatest, memorable spiritual experiences of my adult life. The experience was so spiritually profound that I researched the author because I *immediately* wanted to get and read another book by her. And then I discovered that she's … a little bit … out there. So out there that I became a bit hesitant about reading anything else she wrote. (I *did* buy *Evenings with the Holy Spirit*,[41] but I admit I never read it.) She does conferences and podcasts and has written *lots and lots* of books. She even has her own publishing company.

Yet, the spiritual blessing and experience I received *throughout the course of reading this book* still today remains something I *crave* to experience again. It would be an absolute travesty for you to not read this beautiful, inspirational, blessed book.

Favorite Quote(s):

- "I will work it all – the hurt, the disappointment, the betrayals – together for your good because you love Me and I love you. I will give you beauty for ashes."[42]
- "Jesus is the author and finisher of your faith, and all Father's promises are yes and amen."[43]

---

[41] Jennifer LeClaire, *Evenings With the Holy Spirit: Listening Daily to the Still, Small Voice of God* (Charisma House, 2024).
[42] LeClaire, *Mornings With The Holy Spirit*, 5.

25

- "When you confess My will in the face of an opposite reality, it strengthens your faith. When you commit to waiting to see My glory manifest in your circumstances, you develop the patience that holds up your faith and allows you to inherit the promises you have long hoped to see manifest."[44]

- "Waiting on the Lord is an active pursuit of Father's will. Waiting on the Lord is eagerly expecting Me to show up in the midst of your circumstances to tell you exactly what to do and what to say at a particular time."[45]

- "What you make happen for someone else, We will make happen for you."[46]

- "No matter what comes your way, I am as close to you as you want Me to be."[47]

- "The frustration you feel isn't going to go away unless you change something – either the source of the frustration, your perspective on it, or your attitude toward it."[48]

Book Summary[49]:

Inspiring daily devotionals—prophetic words from the Holy Spirit—to strengthen, comfort, and counsel you.

Many people are crying out to Jesus, but few are regularly fellowshipping with the Holy Spirit. Yet the Holy Spirit dwells in our spirits. We are His temple (1 Cor. 6:19), and He is our Comforter, Counselor, Helper, Intercessor, Advocate, Strengthener and Standby (John 14:26, AMP). The Holy Spirit leads and guides us into all truth—including the truth about our beautiful Savior (John 16:13).

---

[43] LeClaire, 50.
[44] LeClaire, 59.
[45] LeClaire, 147.
[46] LeClaire, 150.
[47] LeClaire, 242.
[48] LeClaire, 297.
[49] All book summaries are cut and pasted from Amazon's website, however each one is the specific book summary put out by each book's publisher.

DAILY DEVOTIONALS

And the Holy Spirit is speaking to us more than we know.

Mornings With the Holy Spirit is a daily devotional written as if the Holy Spirit is speaking directly to you. Through her personal journaling during times of worship, prayer, and just everyday living, Jennifer LeClaire has recorded the words that the Holy Spirit has given her, and she shares them with you in this book. Each entry will include a brief message from the Holy Spirit, a relevant Scripture reference or references, and a prayer starter.

Purchase Tips:

Always tried to buy used! *Always.* My copy of this book was a journal, allowing me to make notes each day but I'm not sure it's available that way anymore.

Author Profile[50]:

I'm Jennifer LeClaire. You might know me as the former editor of Charisma magazine or as the author of books like "The Making of a Prophet," "The Spiritual Warrior's Guide to Defeating Jezebel" or one of another 30 books here on Amazon.

If you are anything like me you have experienced some major challenges in your life. Looking back, I am very thankful for the challenges I have overcome. I learned a great deal from them and they have ultimately made me a better person. I'm getting ahead of myself though!

You might be surprised to learn that I didn't grow up in the church. I was born in Winter Garden, just outside of Orlando, Florida. As a youth, I visited Catholic churches with my neighbors on Easter and Christmas. I remember visiting a Presbyterian church on a military base once.

---

[50] This profile is the author's official biography available on Amazon.

DAILY DEVOTIONALS

I always believed in Jesus, but I didn't come to the Lord until I was 30 years old. I've been sold out to God ever since.

"Faith is the heroic effort of your life."[51]

Oswald Chambers: My Utmost for His Highest[52]

BOOK SNIP

Type:
This is a daily devotional.

Topic Focus:
This book focuses on helping any believer deepen their relationship to the Lord.

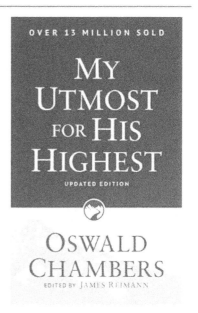

Sue's Thoughts;
Go back decades ago to when bell bottoms were in fashion, Elton John still hadn't come out as gay, and 77WABC was a top of the pops radio station to listen to. I'm talking the late 70s. I was a teen at that time dealing with the usual teen angst issues. Add in the fact that my younger sister had recently died from a terminal illness and I had as of yet not begun to comprehend my personal issues with depression and anxiety. Growing up in a family of faith, God and Jesus and the Holy Spirit and Church and Youth Group and Wednesday Prayer meeting were all integral parts of my life. The wife of our youth minister at our church (she and her husband were only with us for a few months) gifted me a copy of

---

[51] Oswald Chambers, *My Utmost for His Highest* (Uhrichsville, OH: Barbour Publishing, Inc., 1935). May 8th
[52] Chambers.

Oswald Chamber's book, *My Utmost for His Highest* when they were leaving the church. I thought it was the weirdest title and, looking briefly inside, it was written in very "ancient" (think King James Bible) language style.[53]

But once again it was a *pretty* book with gold edges and a dark purple silk bookmark, too. And it was another one that had a little space on each day's page for me to write a little something. The entries are dated so I (of course) began in the middle of the book on the correct date. It was hard reading and I struggled. Something made me read the same short entry again and it was like "DING!" a light went on and I got it! I underlined what I got and then, because I was so excited, I copied down what I had underlined in the journal space. I was so proud of myself, lol.

I would (over a couple of years I admit) read that whole book and, eventually buy a second copy and I read that one again, too.

That Oswald guy knew what he was talking about. He was a minister. After his death, his wife put some of the best bits of his sermons together into this devotional.

Favorite Quote(s):
- "Leave Him to be the source of all your dreams and joys and delights, and go out and obey what He has said."[54]
- "The certainty that I do not know – that is the secret of going with Jesus."[55]
- "Faith never knows where it is being led, but it loves and knows the One Who is leading."[56]

---

[53] You should know that this book is now regularly publishing in "contemporary language" rather than this original style.
[54] Chambers, *My Utmost for His Highest*. Feb. 20th
[55] Chambers. Mar. 9th
[56] Chambers. Mar. 19th

DAILY DEVOTIONALS

- "We are not asked to believe the Bible, but to believe the One Whom the Bible reveals (Jn. 5:39-40). We are called to present liberty of conscience, not liberty of view."[57]
- "All we build is going to be inspected by God."[58]
- "Faith is not intelligent understanding; faith is deliberate commitment to a Person where I see no way."[59]
- "The people who influence us most are not those who buttonhole us and talk to us, but those who live their lives like the stars in heaven and the lilies in the field, perfectly, simply, and unaffectedly. Those are the lives that mold us."[60]
- "Crisis always reveals character."[61]
- "The test of a [person's] religious character is not what he/she does in the exceptional moments of life, but what he/she does in the ordinary times, when there is nothing tremendous or exciting on. The worth of a [person] is revealed in his/her attitude to ordinary things when he/she is not before the footlights."[62]
- "We can all see God in exceptional things, but it requires the culture of spiritual discipline to see God in every detail."[63]

Book Summary[64]:

You'll find 365 thought-provoking meditations in this **updated-language paperback** edition of "the golden book of Oswald

---

[57] Chambers. May 6th
[58] Chambers. May 7th
[59] Chambers. Mar. 28th
[60] Chambers. May 18th
[61] Chambers. Sept. 10th
[62] Chambers. Oct. 12th You might notice quite a bit of "he/she" in this quote as well as inclusive words such as [person] in brackets. Many of these precious books are not gender inclusive and I often catch myself changing them in my head to make it talk more personally to me. I haven't done it for all of the quotes in this book, but when you see words in [brackets] that's me being very presumptuous and altering this famous author's writing. You should try doing it; you'd be amazed at how often the message really personalizes it for you. (If your brave, you can do it with God, too… God is not male…!)
[63] Chambers. Nov. 14th

DAILY DEVOTIONALS

Chambers." My Utmost for His Highest will encourage and move you to think more deeply about your relationship with the Lord.
My Utmost for His Highest has sold over 13 million copies worldwide and is considered one of the most popular religious books ever written. These captivating words of wisdom from Oswald Chambers have challenged and inspired readers for more than 80 years.

Oswald Chambers was a teacher and preacher whose messages cut to the heart of the gospel. His wife, Biddy, transcribed his lectures and sermons and compiled them into books, the most popular being My Utmost for His Highest. The title is taken from a thought in one of his sermons: "Shut out every consideration and keep yourself before God for this one thing only—My Utmost for His Highest."

Chambers was a man completely devoted to Christ, and his life and writings clearly portray that. This daily devotional has inspired countless people to drink deeply from the biblical truths that Chambers so passionately championed.

Purchase Tips:
Always tried to buy used! *Always.*

Author Profile[65]:
Oswald Chambers was converted in his teen years by the ministry of Charles Spurgeon. Chambers studied art and archaeology before answering the call to Christian ministry. Author of the bestseller My Utmost for His Highest, Chambers has more than thirty other titles to his credit, all but one compiled by his wife, Gertrude.

---

[64] All book summaries are cut and pasted from Amazon's website, however each one is the specific book summary put out by each book's publisher.
[65] This profile is the author's official biography available on Amazon.

DAILY DEVOTIONALS

"You were made for paradise. The joys you taste now are infinitesimal compared to those that await you..."[66]

Ann Spangler & Jean Syswerda: Women of the Bible

BOOK SNIP

Type:
This is a daily devotional.

Topic Focus:
This book focuses on fifty-two women in Scripture that we can learn about and learn from – both the "good" and the "bad."

Sue's Thoughts;
This book started it all for me. Seriously. Prior to this book, I was a passionate elementary school teacher and the very blessed stay-at-home mother of three young children. Children were my focus; I never had designs on the adult arena – ever.

I had accepted a parttime job as a children's minister at our church. It was only 15 hours a week, which besides Sunday mornings, were mine to make. It fit my schedule, brought back my teaching joy that I had set aside to be a mom, and added some much-needed money

---

[66] Ann Spangler and Jean E. Syswerda, *Women of the Bible: A One-Year Devotional Study of Women in Scripture* (Grand Rapids, Mich.: Zondervan Publishing House, 1999), 24.

DAILY DEVOTIONALS

into the family finances. I had a blast and developed a close relationship with a much appreciated collection of volunteers that helped everything we instituted become successful.

My mother bought me a copy of this book as a birthday gift in 1999 when I had a 5-year-old, 3-year-old, and a 7-month-old. I honestly was really too busy to read it! I was polite though and made the effort to read the first week's entry (each Bible woman has five entries that are to be read over the course of each week). On the final day of the first woman (Eve, of course) the author concluded with the statement, "You were made for paradise."

I had never considered that. Ever. It was a profoundly intense truth that could not be denied and I was overwhelmed. And it made me cry. I was never the same person after that.

Sometime later, at the local Bible bookstore (I was looking for church materials) what should be on sale but copies of this exact book! Excitedly (because they were a really great price) I bought ten copies with the intention of giving them as thank you gifts to all the women that had been helping me. I took the time to write a note in each one and went around to each house and stuck them in their mailboxes. I was so pleased with myself!

The following Sunday, they all crowded around me and said, "So, when do you want to lead this Bible/book study?"

The rest is history.

Favorite Quote(s):

- [God] "created you in his own image, making you a woman capable of reflecting his love, truth, strength, goodness, wisdom, and beauty."[67]

---

[67] Spangler and Syswerda, 24.

- "No matter what your given name, God knows it. In love, he calls you to him by your name, and you belong to him (Is. 43:1).[68]
- "Jesus told us to remember that as believers we are the salt of the earth… Our attitudes and actions can cleanse and season and purify our surroundings."[69]
- "Praise God that though he hates sin he also loves mercy."[70]
- "If a woman like Miriam could act in a way so displeasing to God, certainly we, too, are capable of sinning, no matter what we have done for him in the past."[71]
- "Faith, after all, is what your life and the vitality of your relationship with God depend on."[72]
- For Martha, "Perhaps this competent woman realized for the first time just how much she had been missing."[73]
- "Offer thanks for the benefits of wisdom you have already tasted in your daily life."[74]
- "So often God uses the most unlikely characters to fulfill his purposes."[75]
- "Wisdom has nothing to do with how many "gray cells" you possess. You can be smart as a whip but still full of foolishness."[76]
- "God called the wise woman of Abel to act, and she did… God asks the same obedience of us when he calls. We may hesitate, we may wish to go the other way, we may dodge and shuffle, but in the end we must obey. When we do, we can trust that we don't go alone. God is there, giving us the help and assurance we require."[77]

---

[68] Spangler and Syswerda, 28.
[69] Spangler and Syswerda, 43.
[70] Spangler and Syswerda, 46.
[71] Spangler and Syswerda, 99.
[72] Spangler and Syswerda, 106.
[73] Spangler and Syswerda, 365.
[74] Spangler and Syswerda, 272.
[75] Spangler and Syswerda, 263.
[76] Spangler and Syswerda, 199.

DAILY DEVOTIONALS

Book Summary[78]:

Women of the Bible focuses on fifty-two remarkable women in Scripture -- women whose struggles to live with faith and courage are not unlike our own. Far from being cardboard characters, these women encourage us through their failures as well as their successes. You'll see how God acted in surprising and wonderful ways to draw them -- and you -- to himself. This year-long devotional offers a unique method to help you slow down and savor the story of God's unrelenting love for his people, offering a fresh perspective that will nourish and strengthen your personal communion with him.

Purchase Tips:

Always tried to buy used! *Always.*

Author Profile[79]:

Ann Spangler is an award-winning author, publishing her first book, an instant bestseller, in 1994. Since then, she has gone on to write several bestselling books, including Women of the Bible (co-authored with Jean Syswerda), Praying the Names of God, Praying the Names of Jesus, and Sitting at the Feet of Rabbi Jesus (co-authored with Lois Tverberg). Her latest book is Less Than Perfect. Together her books have sold millions of copies.

In 2013 she was named the Logos Bookstore Author of the Year, an award given to an author "whose body of works exemplifies the power of books to change lives forever."

By paying attention to the spiritual and emotional hungers that animate us and by finding creative ways to explore God's self-revelation in Scripture, her writing surprises by revealing a God who is often far bigger and better than we might imagine.

---

[77] Spangler and Syswerda, 198.
[78] All book summaries are cut and pasted from Amazon's website, however each one is the specific book summary put out by each book's publisher.
[79] This profile is the author's official biography available on Amazon.

DAILY DEVOTIONALS

In addition to writing, Ann has enjoyed a lengthy career in Christian publishing, working for William B. Eerdmans Publishing Company, Servant Publications, and Zondervan Publishing in marketing, editorial, and management roles. Her broad experience in publishing has convinced her that readers are looking for well-written books that explore the connection between spiritual experience and everyday life, books that both engage the mind and strengthen the heart.

DAILY DEVOTIONALS

Brian D. McClaren: We Make the Road By Walking[81]

BOOK SNIP

Type:
This is a daily devotional.

Topic Focus:
A book that seeks to make every believer more aware of not only the world around us but the impact we have within it.

Sue's Thoughts;
This is my newest devotional and I'll be honest with you; I haven't finished it yet. Assigned by one of this semester's seminary professors,[82] it's one of those devotionals that can be read in any order. In our course, we've been assigned random chapters so I've kind of gone all over.

Each entry gives Scripture to read, and some brief pages of thought by the author. At the end of each entry are a number of questions that you can discuss personally or with a group. The entries invite discussion on a variety of important, current, sometimes difficult

---

[80] Brian D. McLaren, *We Make the Road by Walking: A Year Long Quest for Spiritual Formation, Reorientation, and Activation* (New York: Jericho Books, 2015), 235.
[81] McLaren, *We Make the Road by Walking: A Year Long Quest for Spiritual Formation, Reorientation, and Activation.*
[82] Hi, Dr. Janice!!!!

DAILY DEVOTIONALS

topics that must be faced by believers and searchers alike.[83] I particularly like this book because it addresses *real* situations and struggles that humanity is facing *today*.

It's another one of those books that I've underlined and starred and turned over corners and even begun buying copies to give as gifts. It would be a valuable additional to your devotional library.

Favorite Quote(s):

- "To be alive means to bear responsibility the image of God."[84]
- "Faith is stepping of the map of what's known and making a new road by walking into the unknown."[85]
- "Whenever we engage with the stories of the Bible, we become members of the interpretive community."[86]
- "What if the [impossible stories of the Bible] are meant to challenge us to blur the lines between what is possible and what we think is impossible?"[87]
- "True aliveness focuses on *transforming our deeper desires*."[88]
- "Paul constantly reminds us that all people have equal dignity in Christ; male or female, slave or free, Jew, Greek, Roman or foreigner."[89]
- "God doesn't give us short cuts around hardships, but strengthens us through them."[90]
- "The Spirit will draw you to use your vote and your power for those who aren't at the table of privilege…"[91]

---

[83] I don't like to use the term "non-believers." I believe everyone is a searcher regarding God in some way – whether they realize it or not.
[84] McLaren, *We Make the Road by Walking: A Year Long Quest for Spiritual Formation, Reorientation, and Activation*, 7.
[85] McLaren, 24.
[86] McLaren, 51.
[87] McLaren, 66.
[88] McLaren, 133.
[89] McLaren, 188.
[90] McLaren, 197.

- "Sooner or later everyone should be arrested or imprisoned for a good cause."[92]
- "...death simply means leaving the presence of God in this little neighborhood of history called the present...we join God in the vast, forever expanding future, into which both past and present are forever taken up."[93]
- "...try to imagine that this great, big, beautiful goodness, wholeness and aliveness into which all of us and all of creation will be taken up..."[94]

Book Summary[95]:

From critically acclaimed author Brian McLaren comes a brilliant retelling of the biblical story and a thrilling reintroduction to Christian faith.

This audiobook offers everything you need to explore what a difference an honest, living, growing faith can make in our world today. It also puts tools in your hands to create a life-changing learning community in any home, restaurant, or other welcoming space.

The 52 (plus a few) weekly readings can each be read aloud in 10-12 minutes, and offer a simple curriculum of insightful reflections and transformative practices. Organized around the traditional church year, these readings give an overview of the whole Bible and guide an individual or a group of friends through a year of rich study, interactive learning, and personal growth.

---

[91] McLaren, 232.
[92] McLaren, 260.
[93] McLaren, 249.
[94] McLaren, 259.
[95] All book summaries are cut and pasted from Amazon's website, however each one is the specific book summary put out by each book's publisher.

DAILY DEVOTIONALS

Perfect for home churches, congregations, classes, or individual study, each reading invites you to:

Cultivate an honest, intelligent understanding of the Bible and of Christian faith in the 21st century

Engage with discussion questions designed to challenge, stimulate, and encourage

Re-imagine what it means to live joyfully and responsibly in today's world as agents of God's justice, creativity, and peace

If you're seeking a fresh way to experience and practice your faith, if you're a long-term Christian seeking new vitality, or if you feel out of place in traditional church circles, this audiobook will inspire and activate you in your spiritual journey.

Purchase Tips:
Always tried to buy used! *Always.*

Author Profile:
Brian D. McLaren is an author, a speaker, an activist, and a public theologian. After teaching college English, Brian was a church planter and pastor in the Baltimore-Washington, D.C., area for over twenty years. He is a popular conference speaker and a frequent guest lecturer for denominational and ecumenical leadership gatherings in the United States and internationally, and is the theologian-in-residence at Life in the Trinity Ministry.[96]

---

[96] McLaren, *We Make the Road by Walking: A Year Long Quest for Spiritual Formation, Reorientation, and Activation.* This is the "About the Author" inside the text.

DAILY DEVOTIONALS

Wise men and women are always learning,
always listening for fresh insights.[97]
Proverbs 18:15

BOOKS TO READ

---

[97] Peterson, *The Message: The Bible In Contemporary Language.*

BOOKS TO READ

"Losing yourself in love really is the best thing in the world – and out of it. It is what the doctrine of the Trinity is about..."[98]

Jeffrey John: The Meaning In the Miracles[99]

BOOK SNIP

Type:
This is a text to be read.

Topic Focus:
The author takes the very familiar miracles of Jesus and provides profound insight from historical and cultural knowledge to offer a richer, deeper understanding of Jesus' intent and purpose.

Sue's Thoughts;
This book is in a class all by itself. You will be a different believer of Jesus' miracles should you read it. Unfortunately, it is somewhat difficult to obtain.[100]

---

[98] Jeffrey John, *The Meaning in the Miracles* (Grand Rapids, Mich.: William B. Eerdmans Publishing Company, 2001), 53.

[99] John, *The Meaning in the Miracles.*

[100] This book was originally published in the UK and when we studied it in our Bible study group we were only able to obtain used copies – nothing new. I DID get a Kindle e-copy, however! It's worth the trouble and the used copies *were not expensive.*

Jeffrey John takes nineteen of Jesus' miracles and, providing Scriptural reference, he retells them. He then provides fascinating commentary that addresses cultural and historical issues, Greek and Hebrew insight, and other perceptions which provide fascinating new depth and meaning to the miracle being discussed. Finally, he brings the message and the purpose of the biblical account *forward* to us - "The Meaning for Today" welcoming these insights into our contemporary setting.

I read this book first on my own and talked so much about it in our study group that everyone finally said, "Why don't we do it together?"

It is particularly precious that all of these familiar miracle stories (some of which we have been hearing since we were children) suddenly take on an *entirely new dimension* for us and those we are witnessing to.

I can't say enough about this book.

Favorite Quote(s):

- "Jesus is shown doing something that in his own day was unthinkable for a devout Jew, let alone a rabbi."[101]
- "The only truly Christian form of resistance is prayerful, non-violent witness and protest – in the firm faith that even the powers, however warped and fallen they may be, are ultimately creatures of God, and are ultimately redeemable by his love."[102]
- "Faith is not yet union with God, or even vision. But it is an opening up, a willed act of trust and hope that lets God in through the closed barrier of self."[103]

---

[101] John, *The Meaning in the Miracles*, 92.
[102] John, 92.
[103] John, 39.

- "Every organization or community as well as every individual has its corporate 'demon' – that is, its spiritual as well as worldly aspect; and its potential for generating good or evil will depend on whether it is ordered according to God's will or against it. All systems and societies are therefore capable of becoming demonic in the worst sense."[104]
- "Prayer … is the opposite of self-reliance; a reliance on God which actively seeks his help."[105]
- "Jesus…constant[ly] refus[es] to approach or judge people as members of a class, face, sex or category of any kind, but only as an individual. He deals with the human being, ignoring the label, and this is the heart of Jesus' 'inclusivity.'"[106]
- "Thankfulness goes a step further than faith… Faith is only the beginning of relationship; it expresses belief and trust in its object."[107]
- "The church did not develop or perpetuate the liberating attitude that characterizes Jesus' treatment of women in the Gospels."[108]

Book Summary[109]:

Many explanations of the miracles recorded in the Gospels fall into one of two questionable categories: unthinking acceptance or debunking, which leaves only some vague moral lessons to be learned. In this text, Jeffery John sets the miracles of Jesus in a wider biblical context and shows them to be loaded with theological and prophetic relevance. This broad perspective, which brings together theological enquiry and the needs of personal faith, should come as a

---

[104] John, 15–16.
[105] John, 148.
[106] John, 160.
[107] John, 180.
[108] John, 207–8.
[109] All book summaries are cut and pasted from Amazon's website, however each one is the specific book summary put out by each book's publisher.

revelation to many Christians searching for a proper understanding of Jesus' miracles.

Purchase Tips:
Always tried to buy used! *Always.*

Author Profile:
"Jeffrey John is the newly appointed Dean of St. Alban's Cathedral in Hertfordshire, England. In his work and his writing he is concerned to bridge the gulf between academic theology and local church life.[110]

---

[110] John, *The Meaning in the Miracles.* This was copied from the text's back cover.

BOOKS TO READ

"God is always the God of surprises."[111]

N. T. Wright: Surprised by Hope[112]

BOOK SNIP

Type:
This is a text to be read.

Topic Focus:
N.T. Wright works to revitalize the original, radical understanding of resurrection, salvation, and the Good News of Christ's message regarding the Kingdom of God and what believers have to hope for. I found this book to be unique, surprising, and exciting with its

insights. My understanding and expectation of heaven will never be the same as a result of this book.

Sue's Thoughts;
This is another one of those books that has been transformational for me. N.T. Wright is another prolific author that has podcasts and online classes and extensive written works to read. You may have heard of him or already read one of his other very famous books. He

---

[111] N. T. Wright, *Surprised by Hope: Rethinking Heaven, the Resurrection, and the Mission of the Church*, 1st ed (New York: HarperOne, 2008), 184.
[112] Wright, *Surprised by Hope*.

is a scholar, so some of his work is quite deep, but that should not discourage you from reading this.

I read this book as part of my seminary course on the Afterlife[113] and it focuses on the promise of life after death. Using Scripture and scholarly research, Wright peals back much of the confusion and misunderstanding of what all this talk about heaven, resurrection, eternal life, the second coming, etc. is all about.

It *does not* provide you with a solid, concrete understanding or description so that you can shut the book and say, "So *that's* what it is going to be exactly like!" What it does do, however, (as the title suggests), is provide a blessed hope of what the Bible *does* promise and what Jesus Christ *did* share in his Gospel message. Reading it gave me wonderful new clarity and insight (I can't tell you how many times I wrote "WOW" in the margins) so that we can have a greater understanding of what all this "on earth as it is in heaven" business is all about.

Talk about hope!

Favorite Quote(s):

- "...the traditional picture of people going to either heaven or hell as a one-stage postmortem journey (with or without the option of some kind of purgatory or continuing journey as an intermediate stage) represents a serious distortion and diminution of the Christian hope."[114]

- "All the skills and talents we have put to God's service in this present life – and perhaps too the interests and likings we gave up because they conflicted with our vocation – will be enhanced and ennobled and given back to us to be exercised to his glory."[115]

---

[113] Hi, Dr. Rix!!
[114] Wright, *Surprised by Hope*, 148.
[115] Wright, 161.

- "Since both the departed saints and we ourselves are in Christ, we share with them in the "communion of saints." They are still our brothers and sisters in Christ. When we celebrate the Eucharist, they are there with us, along with the angels and archangels."[116]

- "God is utterly committed to set the world right in the end. This doctrine, like that of resurrection itself, is held firmly in place by the belief in God as creator, on the one side, the belief in his goodness, on the other. And that setting right must necessarily involve the elimination of all that distorts God's good and lovely creation and in particular of all that defaces his image-bearing human creatures."[117]

- "It is the story of God's kingdom being launched on earth as in heaven, generating a new state of affairs in which the power of evil has been decisively defeated, the new creation has been decisively launched, and Jesus's followers have been commissioned and equipped to put that victory and that inaugurated new world into practice."[118]

- "You are not oiling the wheels of a machine that's about to roll over a cliff. You are not restoring a great painting that's shortly going to be thrown on the fire. You are not planting roses in a garden that's about to be dug up for a building site. You are – strange though it may seem, almost as hard to believe as the resurrection itself – accomplishing something that will become in due course part of God's new world. Every act of love, gratitude, and kindness; every work of art or music inspired by the love of God and delight in the beauty of his creation; every minute spent teaching a severely handicapped child to read or to walk; every act of care and nurture, of comfort and support, for one's fellow human beings and for that matter one's fellow nonhuman creatures; and of course every prayer, all Spirit – led teaching,

---

[117] Wright, 179.
[118] Wright, 204.

BOOKS TO READ

every deed that spreads the gospel, builds up the church, embraces and embodies holiness rather than corruption, and makes the name of Jesus honored in the world – all of this will find its way, through the resurrecting power of God, into the new creation that God will one day make. That is the logic of the mission of God."[119]

- "…people who believe in the resurrection, in God making a whole new world in which everything will be set right at last, are unstoppably motivated to work for that new world in the present."[120]

Book Summary[121]:

Renowned Bible scholar, Anglican bishop, and best-selling author N. T. Wright argues that Christians have not distorted the Bible's message about heaven and what happens after we die.

For years, Christians have been asking, "If you died tonight, do you know where you would go?" It turns out that many believers have been giving the wrong answer. It is not heaven.

Wright outlines the present confusion about a Christian's future hope and shows how it is deeply intertwined with how we live today. Wright asserts that Christianity's most distinctive idea is bodily resurrection, and provides a magisterial defense for a literal resurrection of Jesus. Wright then explores our expectation of "new heavens and a new earth", revealing what happens to the dead until then and what will happen with the "second coming" of Jesus. For many, including many Christians, it will come as a great surprise to learn that heaven comes to earth instead of us going to heaven.

---

[119] Wright, 208.
[120] Wright, 214.
[121] All book summaries are cut and pasted from Amazon's website, however each one is the specific book summary put out by each book's publisher.

BOOKS TO READ

Wright convincingly argues that what we believe about life after death directly affects what we believe about life before death. For if God intends to renew the whole creation - and if this has already begun in Jesus's resurrection - the church cannot stop at "saving souls" but must anticipate the eventual renewal by working for God's kingdom in the wider world, bringing healing and hope in the present life.

Author Profile[122]:

N.T. WRIGHT is the former Bishop of Durham in the Church of England and one of the world's leading Bible scholars. He is now serving as the Chair of New Testament and Early Christianity at the School of Divinity at the University of St. Andrews. For twenty years he taught New Testament studies at Cambridge, McGill and Oxford Universities. As being both one of the world's leading Bible scholars and a popular author, he has been featured on ABC News, Dateline, The Colbert Report, and Fresh Air. His award-winning books include The Case for the Psalms, How God Became King, Simply Jesus, After You Believe, Surprised by Hope, Simply Christian, Scripture and the Authority of God, The Meaning of Jesus (co-authored with Marcus Borg), as well as being the translator for The Kingdom New Testament. He also wrote the impressive Christian Origins and the Question of God series, including The New Testament and the People of God, Jesus and the Victory of God, The Resurrection of the Son of God and most recently, Paul and the Faithfulness of God.

Purchase Tips:

This book has been available for purchase since 1989 and is available in various formats. It can be easily purchased used for a very affordable cost. I found my used copy for only $5.00!

---

[122] This profile is the author's official biography available on Amazon.

"God is easy to please, but hard to satisfy."[123]

C.S. Lewis: Mere Christianity[124]

BOOK SNIP

Type:
This is a text to be read.

Topic Focus:
This book discusses the core beliefs of Christianity working to give interesting analogies to help understand complex theological concepts.

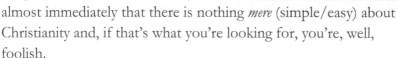

Sue's Thoughts;
First off, the title "Mere" Christianity is a play on words. Lewis tells you almost immediately that there is nothing *mere* (simple/easy) about Christianity and, if that's what you're looking for, you're, well, foolish.

Lewis is another scholar and I will admit that I read this book slowly over a lengthy period of time and kept a notebook by my side to write notes. (I'm thinking of the phrase, "How do you eat an elephant? *One bite at a time.)* But oh, what a meal you will end up with!

Lewis is an *apologist*. An apologist is someone who likes to offer an argument (often in simple, easy to understand terms) that proves or

[123] C. S. Lewis, *Mere Christianity*, Revised&Enlarged edition (San Francisco: HarperOne, 2023), 161.
[124] Lewis, *Mere Christianity*.

BOOKS TO READ

defends something that can be viewed as controversial. You know like being filled with the Holy Spirit and transformed into a completely new creature ... and stuff like that. He works to take divine concepts (of which he readily admits cannot be understood by the human mind) and break them down into concrete, kind-of tangible examples. As I read and took my notes, I began to drawn pictures in my notes because it was those (sometimes funny) analogies that kept making me go, "OOOOOHHH! Now I get it!" In the end, I would lead a Bible study (with its own study booklet) that I called C.S. Lewis & Me: Mere Christianity in Pictures.[125] His analogies work a lot like Jesus' parables were meant to work; they are easy to remember and simplify complex divine concepts so that our tiny brains can understand some of it.

Here's an example. Lewis talked about the importance of marriage and used an analogy I loved. He said that in a good marriage, the kind that God intended, the two who become one should be like a lock and a key. Separately, each piece is vital but together they are so much more effective. Doesn't that make a good picture in your head? Doesn't that make good sense?

C.S. Lewis' book, would make me a different believer by challenging me, providing me with insight, and giving me better tools to explain why I believe what I believe.

But it wasn't simple or easy.

Favorite Quote(s):

- "All decent human beings have an idea that they must behave a certain way. None of us human beings behave the way we should." [126]

---

[125] Susan Lee McGeown, C.S. Lewis & Me: Mere Christianity In Pictures (CreateSpace Independent Publishing Platform, 2013).
[126] Lewis, Mere Christianity. All quotes here are from the text, but I have so many copies I do not know exactly what page they can be found. SORRY.

- "You can shut Him up for a fool, you can spit at Him and kill Him as a demon; or you can fall at His feet and call Him Lord and God. But let us not come with any patronizing nonsense about His being a great human teacher. He has not left that open to us. He did not intend to."[127]

- "As long as you are proud you cannot know God. A proud [person] is always looking down on things and people: and of course, as long as you are looking down, you cannot see something that is above you."[128]

- "Human beings judge one another by their external actions. God judges them by their moral choices."[129]

- "God is not hurried along in the Time-stream of this universe any more than an author is hurried along in the imaginary time of his/her own novel. He/She has infinite attention to spare for each one of us. He/She does not have to deal with us in the mass. You are as much along with Him as if you were the only being He had ever created. When Christ died, He died for you individually just as much as if you had been the only [person] in the world."[130]

- "Very often, the only way to get a quality in reality is to start behaving as if you had it already."[131]

Book Summary[132]:

Mere Christianity explores the core beliefs of Christianity by providing an unequaled opportunity for believers and nonbelievers alike to hear a powerful, rational case for the Christian faith. A brilliant collection, Mere Christianity remains strikingly fresh for the

---

[127] Lewis, 51.

[128] Lewis, 105.

[129] Lewis, 80.

[130] Lewis, 138. Here is my presumptuous/inclusive gender change again…forgive me, C.S.

[131] Lewis, 151.

[132] All book summaries are cut and pasted from Amazon's website, however each one is the specific book summary put out by each book's publisher.

BOOKS TO READ

modern reader and at the same time confirms C. S. Lewis's reputation as one of the leading writer and thinkers of our age.

The book brings together Lewis' legendary broadcast talks during World War II. Lewis discusses that everyone is curious about: right and wrong, human nature, morality, marriage, sins, forgiveness, faith, hope, generosity, and kindness.

Purchase Tips:
Always tried to buy used! *Always.*

This book has been around *forever* and is available inexpensively in all formats (I got my Kindle copy for $1!).

Author Profile[133]:
CLIVE STAPLES LEWIS (1898-1963) was one of the intellectual giants of the twentieth century and arguably one of the most influential writers of his day. He was a fellow and tutor in English Literature at Oxford University until 1954 when he was unanimously elected to the Chair of Medieval and Renaissance English at Cambridge University, a position he held until his retirement. He wrote more than thirty books, allowing him to reach a vast audience, and his works continue to attract thousands of new readers every year. His most distinguished and popular accomplishments include Mere Christianity, Out of the Silent Planet, The Great Divorce, The Screwtape Letters, and the universally acknowledged classics, the Chronicles of Narnia. To date, the Narnia books have sold over 100 million copies and been transformed into three major motion pictures.

---

[133] This profile is the author's official biography available on Amazon.

"Simply labeling one's ideas "theology" does not guarantee that they represent the mind of God."[134]

Lynn Japinga: Feminism and Christianity[135]

BOOK SNIP

Type:
This is a text to be read.

Topic Focus:
As the title suggestions, this book explores the question can a woman be a feminist and a Christian? Japinga works to prove the answer is a resounding *yes*.

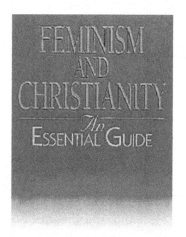

Sue's Thoughts;
If you know me, you know that my opinions on gender equality both inside and outside of religious settings has always been important to me. So, it's no wonder that I've got this book on my shelf, right?

This book offers in solid yet understandable language how feminism and Christianity indeed fit together. Using Scripture, Japinga breaks down the hows and whys of how religion has and has not been on the right track in regard to women and men.

---

[134] Lynn Japinga, *Feminism and Christianity: The Essential Guide* (Nashville, TN: Abingdon Press, 1999), 19.
[135] Japinga, *Feminism and Christianity: The Essential Guide*.

Nothing that she talks about was new, per se. Everything she talks about I already believed, but she provided me with an extensive collection of rational, biblically based truths that help me sound more erudite and not just like some angry, man-hating woman (which I'm not, by the way). The very first quote I've written for you in this section (about Jesus and Paul) was so profoundly articulated for me that when I first read it, I cried. It still gives me chills and makes me emotional and remains my single most frequently written quote, *ever*. "The liberating elements of the Bible, such as the equality of men and women, the creation of women in God's image, and Jesus' affirmation of women, came from God and thus represent the timeless truths of salvation."[136]

How can one argue with that Truth?

Favorite Quote(s):

- "Jesus and Paul contradicted the Old Testament even though they valued it as God's word. They established a new set of criteria, which made faith and grace the center of Christianity…Scholars call this approach the "canon within the canon," which means that within the accepted canon, or list of writings finally gathered into the Bible, there is a subset of texts that serve as the central theme by which all others must be measured."[137]
- Discerning a central theme requires the reader to make judgments about which parts of the Bible constitute its essential message and which parts represent culturally conditioned advice."[138]
- "…the liberating elements of the Bible, such as the equality of men and women, the creation of women in God's image, and Jesus' affirmation of women, came from God and thus represent the timeless truths of salvation."[139]

---

[136] Japinga, 51.
[137] Japinga, 51.
[138] Japinga, 51.

BOOKS TO READ

- "The Bible has authority in my life because it makes sense of my experience and speaks to me about the meaning and purpose of my humanity in Jesus Christ. In spite of its ancient and patriarchal worldviews, in spite of its inconsistencies and mixed messages, the story of God's love affair with the world leads me to a vision of New Creation that impels my life..."[140]

- "...beliefs are stated with a caution that recognizes that no human being can be absolutely right when making statements about God. Humility is an awareness that God might choose to act in ways that defy the best theories, the recognition that the surprising work of God is not yet finished and that at the end-of-life human beings may be stunned by the grace of God."[141]

- "...the feminist critique of tradition emphasizes that theology is a partial, fallible attempt to say something true and meaningful about the God who transcends all human understanding. Human knowledge is incomplete and at times distorted, which means that human efforts at theology are never complete."[142]

- "The development of feminist consciousness produces a paradigm shift for many women. They begin to look at the world in a different way, and all aspects of their lives are affected... Feminist theologians seek to understand and make sense of this ambiguous Christian faith, which affirms women as God's people and excludes them from the life of the church."[143]

- "Theology does not finally represent the mind of God so much as it illustrates the efforts of human beings to gain a deeper understanding of God, themselves, and the world."[144]

- "...sin must be seen not merely as one individual personal straying away from the values of justice and peace but as a

---

[139] Japinga, 51.
[140] Japinga, 45.
[141] Japinga, 25–26.
[142] Japinga, 25.
[143] Japinga, 20.
[144] Japinga, 19.

BOOKS TO READ

collective, systematic destruction of the community that is at the foundation of God's good creation.[145]

- "Sin has many layers and no one is exempt. Even those who are oppressed may deny others the room to breathe."[146]
- "God's salvation helps people to stand up straight; break free of the rules and expectations that bind them; and live freely, responsibility, and joyfully in the world God has made."[147]

Book Summary[148]:

Some have raised the question: Is it possible, at the same time, to be a Christian and a feminist? Japinga asks the question a bit differently: Is it possible not to be?

Like the other titles in the Essential Guides series, the purpose of this book is simple: to introduce college and seminary students to the basic questions and issues that arise from a feminist interpretation of Christianity. The author explores the central ideas of Christian feminism, including its critique of patriarchy in Christianity and its recovery of the presence, actions, and ideas of women. What has been troublesome in Christianity for feminists and why? How have Christian feminists dealt with these issues? What resources are there in Christianity for the empowering and encouragement of women?

Beginning with an examination of women and the Bible, the book explores biblical texts which define women negatively as well as those which emphasize women's strengths and ability, and then outlines the various feminist approaches to the interpretation of Scripture. It then moves to an overview of women in the history of Christianity and, specifically, of religion in America, presenting both prevailing

---

[145] Japinga, 89.
[146] Japinga, 90.
[147] Japinga, 117.
[148] All book summaries are cut and pasted from Amazon's website, however each one is the specific book summary put out by each book's publisher.

attitudes about women and the (usually unheard) stories of women. After surveying the main questions a feminist method brings to the study of theology, Japinga then explores certain theological questions--How do we speak of God? Who is Christ? What does it mean to be human?

Written from a moderate feminist perspective, this book provides a broad overview of feminist approaches to theological disciplines. It emphasizes consensual scholarship rather than points of controversy. It acquaints students with feminist analysis by way of the central themes common to feminist approaches to several disciplines and introduces readers to this material in ways that lessen the possibility that they will be threatened, intimidated, or angered by it. While the book offers professors an affordable and accessible textbook choice, it is also accessible for lay study groups in congregations.

Purchase Tips:
Always tried to buy used! *Always.*

Author Profile:
Lynn Japinga is Associate Professor of Religion at Hope College, Holland Michigan. An ordained minister in the Reformed Church in America (RCA) she has served as a pastor and interim pastor of a number of RCA congregations. Japinga is the author of several books and articles.[149]

---

[149] Japinga, *Feminism and Christianity: The Essential Guide.* Back cover information.

"Some of God's greatest gifts are unanswered prayers."[150]

Philip Yancey: Prayer – Does It Make A Difference?[151]

BOOK SNIP

Type:
This is a text to be read.

Topic Focus:
Prayer – does it work? Does it work the way we think it does? What can we expect from prayer? Does it change us or God or both?

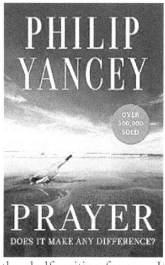

Sue's Thoughts;
I used to be a romance reading fiend. Always had one in progress, and one on the shelf waiting for me. It was my go-to source of entertainment when I had a free moment or two. One spring, my teens came home from school talking about how a lot of their friends had given up things for lent and they wondered if we should do it. I readily agreed.[152] But, being the typical nutty family (and also not Catholic and never having done this before) we gave up rather … interesting things: my oldest son gave up large dinner plates in favor of eating smaller portions on dessert size plates[153] and I gave up … reading romance novels.

---

[150] Philip Yancey, *Prayer - Does It Make Any Difference* (Grand Rapids, Mich.: Zondervan Publishing House, 2006), 230.
[151] Yancey, *Prayer - Does It Make Any Difference*.
[152] Are you kidding?? Teens wanting to do spiritual stuff??? HOORAY.
[153] Which, by the way, we still practice!

BOOKS TO READ

I had this Yancey book on my shelf that someone had given me (for all my spiritual passion, I never was one to read "godly" books very much). So, with no romance book to read (sigh), I began to read it. And it was wonderful.

Yancey is an easy read with interesting quotes highlighted on the pages and easily labeled sections to identify what topics are being covered. And, he writes in a way that touches your heart and your soul and makes you honestly want what he says you can have.

Prayer was never the same for me after reading this book. I would go on to study and read more books on prayer. His statement, "I like to think of my conversations with people as prayer...I willingly refer my actions to God, and in so doing they become a prayer"[154] transformed how I perceived simple conversations or actions with others; allowing them to be holy.

Once again, it was a transformational read that shouldn't be missed.

Favorite Quote(s):

- "We do not pray to tell God what he does not know, nor to remind him of things he has forgotten. He already cares for the things we pray about... He has simply been waiting for us to care about them with him. When we pray, we stand by God and look with him toward those people and problems."[155]

- "I remind myself that the Son of God, who had spoken worlds into being and sustains all that exists, felt a compelling need to pray. He prayed as if it made a difference, as if the time he devoted to prayer mattered every bit as much as the time he devoted to caring for people."[156]

---

[154] Yancey, *Prayer - Does It Make Any Difference*, 314.
[155] Yancey, 58.
[156] Yancey, 79.

- Forget past failures, forget recurring sins, forget feelings of inferiority, and instead open your mind to God, who cannot fill what has not been emptied."[157]
- "God, show me what you are doing today, and how I can be a part of it."[158]
- "I like to think of my conversations with people as prayer…I willingly refer my actions to God, and in so doing they become a prayer."[159]
- "Somehow our love means something incalculable to the God of the universe."[160]

Book Summary[161]:

Philip Yancey probes the very heartbeat of our relationship with God: prayer. What is prayer? Does it change God's mind or ours or both? This book is an invitation to communicate with God the Father who invites us into an eternal partnership through prayer.

Polls reveal that 90 percent of people pray. Yet prayer, which should be the most nourishing and uplifting time of the believer's day, can also be frustrating, confusing, and fraught with mystery.

Writing as a fellow pilgrim, bestselling author of What's So Amazing About Grace? Philip Yancey probes such questions as:

Is God listening?

What should I pray for?

If God knows everything, what's the point of prayer?

---

[157] Yancey, 185.

[158] Yancey, 168. I try to say this prayer every morning before I get out of bed.

[159] Yancey, 314.

[160] Yancey, 322.

[161] All book summaries are cut and pasted from Amazon's website, however each one is the specific book summary put out by each book's publisher.

BOOKS TO READ

If my prayers go unanswered, is there something wrong with my faith?

Why does God sometimes seem close and sometimes seem far away?

How can I make prayer more satisfying?

In this powerful classic of spiritual insight and investigation, Yancey tackles the tough questions about the mystery of prayer and, in the process, comes up with a fresh new approach to this timeless topic.

"I have learned to pray as a privilege, not a duty," writes Yancey, and he invites you to join him on this all-important journey.

Purchase Tips:

Always tried to buy used! *Always.*

Author Profile[162]:

I started my career working as an Editor and then Publisher for Campus Life magazine. During those ten years I learned journalistic skills (there's no tougher audience than teenagers), but every year it seemed I wrote fewer and fewer words. In 1980 my wife and I moved to downtown Chicago where I began a career as a freelance writer. (She has worked as a social worker and hospice chaplain-- which gives me plenty of material to write about!) We lived there until 1992, when we moved to the foothills of Colorado.

I've written over 30 books, most of them still in print, thankfully. Three of them I coauthored with Dr. Paul Brand, who influenced me more than any single person. A recent book, "Fearfully and Wonderfully: The Marvel of Bearing God's Image" is a revised compilation of that content. My other favorites include "Soul Survivor" and "Reaching for the Invisible God" because both of them forced me to dig deep and get personal.

---

[162] This profile is the author's official biography available on Amazon.

BOOKS TO READ

I had two new books released in 2021. "A Companion in Crisis" offers a paraphrase of John Donne's 'Devotions' with commentary and application to our current suffering. My long-awaited memoir, "Where the Light Fell" gives readers a backstory of sorts, revealing the secrets of my turbulent childhood and teen years, and the impact on my written work.

I'm a pilgrim, still 'in recovery' from a bad church upbringing, searching for the possibility of a faith rooted in grace instead of fear. I feel overwhelming gratitude that I can make a living writing about the questions that interest me.

BOOKS TO READ

"Jesus is the Truth and anything that doesn't agree with Jesus is not the Truth."[163]

Keith Giles: Jesus Unbound[164]

BOOK SNIP

Type:
This is a text to be read.

Topic Focus:
This book focuses on establishing an actual relationship with Jesus. It seeks to "liberate the word of God from the Bible." That's because it is Jesus that we must take literally; not the Bible to know God.

Sue's Thoughts;
I don't know how I ended up reading this one. Giles has a lot of books like this title (I have others on my shelf that I'm yet to get to) but I am so glad I started with this one.

Giles is a little bit ... radical. (Not sure that is a good word but he's outspoken and frank about things. Some who have reviewed his writing took issue with some of the things he writes.) He says things like "the Bible is not the word of God," which shocks you but then spends a whole chapter proving that *Jesus* is the Word of God and by

---

[163] Keith Giles, *Jesus Unbound* (Orange, CA: Quoir, 2018), 91.
[164] Giles, *Jesus Unbound*.

BOOKS TO READ

the end you're going, "Yes! I agree!!" all the while your head is exploding.

He will make you think. You'll put the book down and find yourself still thinking about it when you walk away. You'll feel compelled to say to other believers, "What do you think about…?" He will transform (in an important and good way) a lot of misconceptions about what is important in your faith walk and what … just isn't.

I gained a clarity about my faith and what I believed and what I struggled with by reading this book. Giles helped me articulate things that I *knew* but couldn't put into competent explanations. As a result, it made me a more confident believer, witness, and teacher.

It is not an exaggeration to say that I never viewed Scripture or Jesus Christ in the same way after reading this book.

Favorite Quote(s):

- "Only Jesus reveals the Father to us, and Jesus did not reveal to us an angry, wrathful, petty, violent God. He revealed an "Abba" to us who looks just like Jesus in heart and character."[165]
- "…Jesus speaks of a Gospel that is based on an intimate relationship with himself. He talks about the Gospel as being primarily about transformation, no mere information." [166]
- "…if the Gospel is about having the right information, then being right is everything. But, if the Gospel is about transformation, then being Christ-like is everything."[167]
- "…nothing is true unless it lines up with the revelation of Christ. Nothing points the way to God unless it aligns with the teachings of Jesus. Nothing contains the words of life unless those words correspond to the words spoken by Jesus."[168]

---

[165] Giles, 43.
[166] Giles, 59.
[167] Giles, 65.
[168] Giles, 72.

- "As long as we insist upon holding rightly to the rigid inerrancy of the Old Testament scriptures, we will forever be kept from fully embracing the clearest and most accurate portrayal of who God really is."[169]
- "The strongest evidence for the resurrected Christ is the boldness of the disciples, the empty tomb and the failure of Rome or the Jewish leaders to produce the body to silence those who testified that He was alive."[170]

Book Summary[171]:

For many Christians, the Bible is the only way to know anything about God. But according to that same Bible, everyone can know God directly through an actual relationship with Jesus. **Jesus Unbound** is an urgent call for the followers of Jesus to know Him intimately because the Gospel is not mere information about God, but a transformational experience with a Christ who is closer to us than our own heartbeat.

Purchase Tips:

Always tried to buy used! *Always.*

Author Profile[172]:

Keith Giles is a former pastor who left the pulpit to follow Jesus and start a house church where no one takes a salary and 100 percent of all offerings are given to help the poor in the community. He has been a published writer since 1989.

He is the author of several books, including: "Jesus Unbound: Liberating the Word of God from the Bible" and "Jesus Untangled: Crucifying Our Politics To Pledge Allegiance To The Lamb."

---

[169] Giles, 110.
[170] Giles, 183.
[171] All book summaries are cut and pasted from Amazon's website, however each one is the specific book summary put out by each book's publisher.
[172] This profile is the author's official biography available on Amazon.

BOOKS TO READ

Keith is the co-host of the Heretic Happy Hour Podcast which has featured interviews with Bart Ehrman, John Fugelsang, Richard Rohr, Brad Jersak, Greg Boyd, and many others.

Keith also teaches several online courses including "Square 1: From Deconstruction to Reconstruction" and other courses based on his many books.

"While Jesus was foreshadowed *in the old covenant, he did not* come to extend *it. He came to fulfill it, put a bow on it, and* establish something new."[173]

Andy Stanley: Irresistible[174]

BOOK SNIP

Type:
This is a text to be read.

Topic Focus:
What exactly did Jesus present in his ministry that caused a massive transformation of the Jewish community he resided in to believe he was the Son of God? What was it about that early time in the Christian faith that made it practically irresistible?

Sue's Thoughts;
If you find yourself struggling with some (or all) of the aspects of your formal religious denominations rules and regulations, if you find yourself upset with the restrictive and bias policies regarding women, LGBTQ, cultural and/or racial gaps, denominational disunity, etc. then this book is perfect for you.

Andy Stanley (yes, he's Charles Stanley's son[175]) is a gifted speaker (his online sermons are great) and prolific writer. His writing is clear

---

[173] Andy Stanley, *Irresistible - Reclaiming the New That Jesus Unleashed for the World* (Grand Rapids, Mich.: Zondervan Reflective, 2018), 96.
[174] Stanley, *Irresistible - Reclaiming the New That Jesus Unleashed for the World.*

and easy to understand. His purpose with this book is to separate the Gospel message of Jesus Christ and Christ's wish for the church of believers from the religious dogma that has changed and hampered its true purpose. (He and Keith Giles of *Jesus Unbound*[176]*Giles* would do very well together. I wonder if they're friends...?) He's *not* saying abandon all church! What he *is saying* is, "*This* is what Jesus asked for and we must make certain that wherever and whenever believers find themselves, *this* is what we are reflecting ... and nothing else."[177]

I cannot see anything wrong with that goal, can you?

Favorite Quote(s):

- I'm convinced our current versions of the Christian faith need to be stripped of a variety of old covenant leftovers. This has nothing to do with expressions of worship or style. Old is blended with new in modern, traditional, and liturgical churches. We are dragging along a litany of old covenant concepts and assumptions that slow us down, divide us up, and confuse those standing on the outside peering in."[178]

- "What would your brother have to do to convince you he was the Son of God?"[179]

- "Against every Jewish fiber in their Jewish bodies they determined that Gentiles everywhere would have access to the God of *their* fathers without making a single trip to the temple and without sacrificing a single animal. All the benefits, none of the blood. But what's more mind-boggling than that, they decided *unity* in the church was more important than the *law* of Moses."[180]

---

[175] And, just for the record, they don't agree on everything spiritual. I don't know if that is a good thing for you or a bad thing but that's the reality.

[176] Giles, *Jesus Unbound*.

[177] Stanley didn't actually say this...I did. But that's what I got from reading his book.

[178] Stanley, *Irresistible - Reclaiming the New That Jesus Unleashed for the World*, 92.

[179] Stanley, 124.

BOOKS TO READ

- "As inspired as the old covenant may be, it has no, nada, none authority over us, and any effort on our part to wiggle back up underneath its authority is tantamount to declaring the new covenant insufficient."[181]

Book Summary[182]:

Once upon a time there was a version of the Christian faith that was practically irresistible. After all, what could be more so than the gospel that Jesus ushered in? Why, then, isn't it the same with Christianity today?

Author and pastor Andy Stanley is deeply concerned with the present-day church and its future. He believes that many of the solutions to our issues can be found by investigating our roots. In Irresistible, Andy chronicles what made the early Jesus Movement so compelling, resilient, and irresistible by answering these questions:

What did first-century Christians know that we don't—about God's Word, about their lives, about love?

What did they do that we're not doing?

What makes Christianity so resistible in today's culture?

What needs to change in order to repeat the growth our faith had at its beginning?

Many people who leave or disparage the faith cite reasons that have less to do with Jesus than with the conduct of his followers. It's time to hit pause and consider the faith modeled by our first-century brothers and sisters who had no official Bible, no status, and little chance of survival. It's time to embrace the version of faith that

---

[180] Stanley, 130.
[181] Stanley, 160.
[182] All book summaries are cut and pasted from Amazon's website, however each one is the specific book summary put out by each book's publisher.

BOOKS TO READ

initiated—against all human odds—a chain of events resulting in the most significant and extensive cultural transformation the world has ever seen.

This is a version of Christianity we must remember and re-embrace if we want to be salt and light in an increasingly savorless and dark world.

Purchase Tips:
Always tried to buy used! *Always.*

Author Profile[183]:
Communicator, author, and pastor Andy Stanley founded Atlanta-based North Point Ministries (NPM) in 1995. Today, NPM consists of eight churches in the Atlanta area and a network of 180 churches around the globe that collectively serve over 200,000 people weekly.

As host of Your Move with Andy Stanley, which delivers over 10.5 million messages each month through television, digital platforms, and podcasts and author of more than 20 books, including Irresistible; Better Decisions, Fewer Regrets; and Deep & Wide, he is considered one of the most influential pastors in America.

Andy and his wife, Sandra, have three grown children and live near Atlanta.

---

[183] This profile is the author's official biography available on Amazon.

BOOKS TO READ

"Perhaps the greatest irony about his letters is that, in the passages modern readers consider most intolerant, Paul seems, on an examination in context, to be addressing this brutality most humanely."[184]

Sarah Ruden: Paul Among the People[185]

BOOK SNIP

Type:
This is a text to be read.

Topic Focus:
Ruden is an expert scholar in ancient Roman times and the Greek language and culture in general. She brings to life a totally new perspective on what Paul meant in the historical time of his writing.

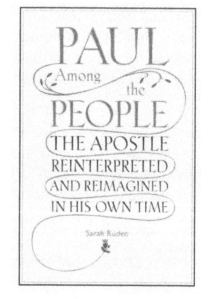

Sue's Thoughts;
Sarah Ruden is an interesting individual. A foremost scholar in ancient Greek, she has translated a number of (apparently) extremely difficult works into English. Then, she decided to explore and translate the ancient writings of the Apostle Paul (probably because there is so much gender controversy over him). (Eventually, she would also decide to tackle translating The Gospels![186])

---

[184] Sarah Ruden, *Paul Among the People* (New York: Image Books, 2010).
[185] Ruden. xvi-xvii.

BOOKS TO READ

She's interesting because, over the course of her life she has decided *not* to be a Christian, but instead is a practicing Quaker.[187] She points this out immediately, which made me read this book (and, yes, I read her *The Gospels* translation, too[188]) initially, very hesitantly.

Paul, initially, was an issue for me, too. I did a conference on Paul, very early on in my speaking career and started out with giving everyone a list of all the truly "obnoxious" stuff that Paul dictates about women in his letters (you know, like we should always wear hats and keep silent in church). Through *my* personal study – without *any* Greek knowledge at all, I was able to reach a point where I came to understand every "obnoxious" thing that Paul said (and it wasn't obnoxious at all).

Ruden does the same thing but she takes it much farther succeeding in proving just *how incredibly progressive and liberating* Paul's messages and edicts are regarding women. Her writing is filled with explanations of the ancient Greek language, culture, and traditions so that when you read Paul's writings in this new context it *all makes glorious* new sense.

(In Ruden's book *The Gospels,* perhaps the most interesting part is her opening chapter in which she explains in detail how she translates, why she translates like she does, and how culture and history play such an important part in the whole process of translating and, consequently, understanding the Bible. Before I even finished the first chapter, I was blown away. After that opening chapter, it's

---

[186] Sarah Ruden, *The Gospels* (New York: Modern Library, 2021).
[187] I know, what's the difference, right? Looking this up on the Internet (Literally: Are Quakers Christian?) doesn't immediately give clarity. Quakers, *on the whole,* reject firm religious dogma, embrace a sort of "universalist perspective" (*much* more inclusive, accepting most religions), and believe that God is in everyone. https://quaker.org/are-quakers-christian/ At least that's what one website said. Ruden's primary issue with Christianity – as with many scholarly women – stemmed in part from the exclusion of women in positions of religious authority.
[188] But reading the Gospels in various translations has always been sort of a hobby for me and I couldn't resist this new, expert translation! I wasn't disappointed.

BOOKS TO READ

"just" the Gospels to read; some of it very familiar and some of it interestingly 'different.')

Regarding BOTH her books, there was not one thing that I read that offended me or put me off as a believer.

Which made me wonder how she could say she was no longer a Christian…

Favorite Quote(s):

- "Rather than repressing women, slaves, or homosexuals, [Paul] made – for his time – progressive rules for the inclusion of all of them in the Christian community, drawing on (but not limited by) traditional Jewish ethics."[189]
- "It is impossible for me to imagine that Paul had plans, or hopes, or even secret fantasies of forcibly repressing people. In his own words I can read only that he tried to persuade them not to start swinging at one another on any excuse."[190]
- "It is no wonder that "inheriting" and "the kingdom of God" go together in scripture. For slaves, freedmen, laborers, soldiers, wanderers, colonists, hucksters, prostitutes (a very large profession), artists, entrepreneurs on a shoestring, and all of the others struggling through the hard facts of the Roman Empire, "inheriting" was a fantasy of salvation."[191]
- "Christianity offered anyone, no matter how poor and powerless, an alternative inheritance… 'We offer you an equal share of a community, such as most of you could only dream of before. You forfeit it only if you are disorderly, through these destructive acts that are not even attractive in comparison to the life you could be leading.' No wonder Christianity grew like mad."[192]

---

[189] Ruden, *Paul Among the People.* xvii.
[190] Ruden, 32.
[191] Ruden, 35.
[192] Ruden, 37.

- "Paul's point…is about two ways of using the body, the one for a life that is worth living forever, the other for a life that is good as death in the short time before it vanishes."[193]
- "I think Paul's rule aimed toward an outrageous equality. All Christian women were to cover their heads in church, without distinction of beauty, wealth, respectability – or of privilege so great as to allow toying with traditional appearances… Perhaps the new decree made independent women of uncertain status, or even slave women, honorary wives in this setting."[194]
- "…real marriage is a secure a part of the Christianity charter, and as different from anything before or since, as the command to turn the other cheek."[195]
- "Love…might be possible if love is not an ethereal, abstract standard, an impossible assignment written in lightning on a rock, but a living God."[196]
- "…only the great gulf, in the eyes of the ancients, between a child and an adult can show the difference between people on their own and people unified with God."[197]

Book Summary[198]:

It is a common—and fundamental—misconception that Paul told people how to live. Apart from forbidding certain abusive practices, he never gives any precise instructions for living. It would have violated his two main social principles: human freedom and dignity, and the need for people to love one another.

Paul was a Hellenistic Jew, originally named Saul, from the tribe of

---

[193] Ruden, 40.
[194] Ruden, 88.
[195] Ruden, 102.
[196] Ruden, 181.
[197] Ruden, 186.
[198] All book summaries are cut and pasted from Amazon's website, however each one is the specific book summary put out by each book's publisher.

BOOKS TO READ

Benjamin, who made a living from tent making or leatherworking. He called himself the "Apostle to the Gentiles" and was the most important of the early Christian evangelists.

Paul is not easy to understand. The Greeks and Romans themselves probably misunderstood him or skimmed the surface of his arguments when he used terms such as "law" (referring to the complex system of Jewish religious law in which he himself was trained). But they did share a language—Greek—and a cosmopolitan urban culture, that of the Roman Empire. Paul considered evangelizing the Greeks and Romans to be his special mission.

"For you were called to freedom, brothers and sisters; only do not use your freedom as an opportunity for self-indulgence, but through love become slaves to one another. For the whole law is summed up in a single commandment, 'You shall love your neighbor as yourself.'"

The idea of love as the only rule was current among Jewish thinkers of his time, but the idea of freedom being available to anyone was revolutionary.

Paul, regarded by Christians as the greatest interpreter of Jesus' mission, was the first person to explain how Christ's life and death fit into the larger scheme of salvation, from the creation of Adam to the end of time. Preaching spiritual equality and God's infinite love, he crusaded for the Jewish Messiah to be accepted as the friend and deliverer of all humankind.

In Paul Among the People, Sarah Ruden explores the meanings of his words and shows how they might have affected readers in his own time and culture. She describes as well how his writings represented the new church as an alternative to old ways of thinking, feeling, and living.

BOOKS TO READ

Ruden translates passages from ancient Greek and Roman literature, from Aristophanes to Seneca, setting them beside famous and controversial passages of Paul and their key modern interpretations. She writes about Augustine; about George Bernard Shaw's misguided notion of Paul as "the eternal enemy of Women"; and about the misuse of Paul in the English Puritan Richard Baxter's strictures against "flesh-pleasing." Ruden makes clear that Paul's ethics, in contrast to later distortions, were humane, open, and responsible.

Paul Among the People is a remarkable work of scholarship, synthesis, and understanding; a revelation of the founder of Christianity.

Purchase Tips:
Always tried to buy used! *Always.*

Author Profile:
Sarah Ruden was educated at the University of Michigan, Johns Hopkins, and Harvard. She has translated five books of classical literature, among them *The Aeneid,* and is the author of *Other Places,* a book of poetry. She is a visiting scholar as Wesleyan University in Middletown, Connecticut, where she lives.[199]

---

[199] Ruden, *Paul Among the People.* This is from the back cover of the text.

"We're always like Jesus and never a jerk. This bias toward ourselves is a huge obstacle..."[200]

Pavlovitz: If God is Love, Don't Be A Jerk[201]

BOOK SNIP

Type:
This is a text to be read.

Topic Focus:
A former pastor, Pavlovitz is sometimes irreverent, but profoundly on point about many of the aspects of the Christian region that are clearly hypocritical.

JOHN PAVLOVITZ

IF GOD IS

LOVE

DON'T BE A

JERK

FINDING A FAITH THAT
MAKES US BETTER HUMANS

Sue's Thoughts;
You know how ministers are not supposed to express their beliefs and are expected to take the middle of the road in sticky subjects such as LGBTQ, politics, immigration, etc.? You know how pastors are not supposed to cause division in their congregations but work continually towards unity, practicing grace and forgiveness for all who they encounter?

Yeah, John Pavlovitz doesn't follow any of that. A former minister, Pavlovitz became disillusioned with the hypocritical attitudes,

---

[200] John Pavlovitz, *If God Is Love Don't Be A Jerk: Finding a Faith That Makes Us Better Humans* (Louisville, KY: Westminster John Knox Press, 2021), 103.
[201] Pavlovitz, *If God Is Love Don't Be A Jerk: Finding a Faith That Makes Us Better Humans.*

BOOKS TO READ

policies, and practices of organized religion and decided, *just as Jesus did*, to call out those religious leaders that did not practice what they preached, live what they admonished, or reflect what Jesus set as a standard. And just like Jesus, he's managed (and continues) to provoke, stir up, and challenge the "powers that be" in both religious, political, and social arenas.

And yet... and yet... He uses Scripture and facts and hard truths that reflect a world that I believe Jesus Christ honestly envisioned. His book is a great read whether you think you will love him or hate him. Honest.

In fact, *if you do hate him*, you would be wise to be just as articulate and informed as he is about religious and political and social issues or he, and everyone else as talented as him, with prove you wrong every single time...with Scriptural Truths.

Favorite Quote(s):

- "Our initial faith traditions are all valid and meaningful. They can give us a working language with which to speak about the mysteries of this life, but whoever and whatever God is doesn't *require* them. Religion ... is always undersized for the task at hand. Religion does its best to give us words for describing something that words aren't ultimately equipped for."[202]
- "People deserve a God who is neither white nor male nor cisgender, nor heterosexual nor Republican because any other God isn't big enough to bear the title or merit any reverence."[203]
- "...fear burns up what we *say* we believe and reveals what we *actually* believe."[204]

---

[202] Pavlovitz, 18.
[203] Pavlovitz, 29.
[204] Pavlovitz, 31.

BOOKS TO READ

- "Fear shouts our convictions with bullhorn force: all the pretense falls away and the veneers crumble and the costumes dissolve and people see us as we really are."[205]

- "...the most untenable, terrifying times likely won't destroy us physically, they will surely define us morally..."[206]

- "...if you're moving with honesty in the journey of meaning, you don't end up knowing more along the way, you simply learn how little you've understood to this point, how much you've gotten wrong in the past, and you grow more reverent and aware of the wonder just beyond the measurable things."[207]

- "...faith isn't about surety but about suspicions; it is an aspirational orientation, a movement toward something just slightly out of reach, something that propels you to ask and seek and know – because you don't know it all yet. There is nothing organized or neat or easy about this, so we should all invite the chaos in, make friends with it, learn to live with it, and see the imperfect process of coexisting with it as a holy act itself."[208]

- "...*Am I trying to understand this person, or am I trying to defeat them? Am I burdened to show them something I've seen or experienced that they haven't or to show them how much smarter or more enlightened I am? Am I genuinely seeking to change their hears – or am I trying to make them feel like an a—hole?*"[209]

- "...does a single-gendered God make any sense, and does it yield a more equitable world and a more loving religion?[210]

- "If God is God-sized, than God can be father, maker, shepherd, mother, guide or friend. God has great range and can't be typecast – and degendering God altogether might be really helpful if we can manage it."[211]

---

[205] Pavlovitz, 31.
[206] Pavlovitz, 33.
[207] Pavlovitz, 44.
[208] Pavlovitz, 45–46.
[209] Pavlovitz, 49.
[210] Pavlovitz, 61.

BOOKS TO READ

- "Jesus' life as witnessed in the Gospel stories was a beautifully subversive manifesto of smallness and kindness and goodness, continually reiterating the sacredness of sacrifice, the dignity of humility, the redemptive nature of forgiveness."[212]
- "Nonreligious people accurately see that pushing someone away is a fairly terrible method of pointing them toward something supposedly life-giving; that wounding them while inviting them into a painful place and then condemning them because they rightly reject it seems like a perverse form of abuse."[213]
- "We Christians can't help but read the Gospels so they skew our way, which is why, in the stories we encounter there, we almost always imagine that we're Jesus – or at the very least, that we're the earnest, faithful disciples alongside him and never the self-righteous religious frauds whose hypocrisy he's condemning."
- "The Bible isn't a textbook. It isn't a formula. It is a complex, nebulous collection of stories that we are invited to explore as we seek to understand this life and the life beyond. It requires faith and wonder and digging and discernment, and peace with paradox and comfort with unknowns."[214]

Book Summary[215]:

Thou Shalt Not Be Horrible.

Imagine for a moment what the world might look like if we as people of faith, morality, and conscience actually aspired to this mantra.

What if we were fully burdened to create a world that was more loving and equitable than when we arrived?

---

[211] Pavlovitz, 62–63.
[212] Pavlovitz, 69.
[213] Pavlovitz, 90.
[214] Pavlovitz, 116.
[215] All book summaries are cut and pasted from Amazon's website, however each one is the specific book summary put out by each book's publisher.

BOOKS TO READ

What if we invited one another to share in wide-open, fearless, spiritual communities truly marked by compassion and interdependence?

What if we daily challenged ourselves to live a faith that simply made us better humans?

John Pavlovitz explores how we can embody this kinder kind of spirituality where we humbly examine our belief system to understand how it might compel us to act in less-than-loving ways toward others.

This simple phrase, "Thou Shalt Not Be Horrible," could help us practice what we preach by creating a world where:

spiritual community provides a sense of belonging where all people are received as we are;

the most important question we ask of a religious belief is not Is it true? but rather, is it helpful?

it is morally impossible to pledge complete allegiance to both Jesus and America simultaneously;

the way we treat others is the most tangible and meaningful expression of our belief system.

In If God Is Love, Don't Be a Jerk, John Pavlovitz examines the bedrock ideas of our religion: the existence of hell, the utility of prayer, the way we treat LGBTQ people, the value of anger, and other doctrines to help all of us take a good, honest look at how the beliefs we hold can shape our relationships with God and our fellow humans—and to make sure that love has the last, loudest word.

Purchase Tips:
Always tried to buy used! *Always.*

Author Profile[216]:

John Pavlovitz is a pastor, writer, and activist from Wake Forest, North Carolina.

In the past four years his blog Stuff That Needs To Be Said has reached a diverse worldwide audience. A 20-year veteran in the trenches of local church ministry, John is committed to equality, diversity, and justice.

In 2017 he released his first book A Bigger Table: Building Messy, Authentic, and Hopeful Spiritual Community, and his forthcoming book Hope and Other Superpowers: A Life-Affirming, Love-Defending, Butt-Kicking, World-Saving Manifesto, arrives November 6th, 2018.

---

[216] This profile is the author's official biography available on Amazon.

"Strong faith in a weak branch is fatally inferior to weak faith in a strong branch."[217]

Timothy Keller: The Reason for God[218]

BOOK SNIP

Type:
This is a text to read.

Topic Focus:
This book focuses on the top ten reasons to doubt Christianity and the top ten reasons to embrace Christianity. It is a valuable read for believers as well as nonbelievers.

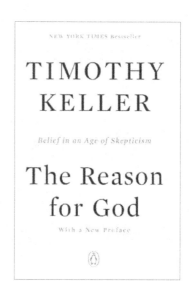

Sue's Thoughts;
This book is one that every Christian should read, hands down. It is divided into two parts: The Leap of Doubt and The Reasons for Faith. Keller, in easy but Scriptural sound writing, addresses both the reasons you *shouldn't doubt* specific things about the Christian faith as well as the reasons you *absolutely must* embrace Christianity as the one faith that has the best answers.

Using Scripture and solid, scholarly reasoning, Keller works to dissect such doubts such as: "There Can't Be Just *One* True Religion," "How Could a Good God Allow Suffering?" and "Science Has Disproved

[217] Tim Keller, *The Reason for God* (New York: Riverhead Books, 2008), 245.
[218] Keller, *The Reason for God*.

BOOKS TO READ

Christianity."[219] The second part of the book focuses on the reasons we *need* to have faith: "The Clues of God," "The (True) Story of the Cross," and "The Dance of God."[220]

His reasoning is simple, sound, and scripturally profound helping not only *your* own personal doubts and questions as well as reinforcing why you have chosen to believe what you believe. For me, it provided blessed insight and inspiration. I felt that it prepared me in better ways to not only be a better witness but a better teacher as well.

Favorite Quote(s):

- "It would be inconsistent to require more justification for Christian believe than you do for you own, but that is frequently what happens…"[221]
- "You must doubt your doubts."[222]
- "Sin is: in despair not wanting to be oneself before God…Faith is: that the self in being itself and wanting to be itself is grounded transparently in God."[223]
- "Forgiveness means bearing the cost instead of making the wrong doer do it, so you can reach out in love to seek your enemy's renewal and change. Forgiveness means absorbing the debt of the sin yourself."[224]
- "The pattern of the Cross means that the world's glorification of power, might, and status is exposed and defeated. On the Cross Christ wins through losing, triumphs through defeat, achieves power through weakness and service, comes to wealth via giving all away. Jesus turns the values of the world upside down."[225]

---

[219] There are a total of seven doubts that Keller addressed.
[220] Again, there are a total of seven reasons that Keller addressed.
[221] Keller, *The Reason for God*. xix
[222] Keller. xix
[223] Keller, 168.
[224] Keller, 199.
[225] Keller, 202–3.

- "Sin is the despairing refusal to find your deepest identity in your relationship and service to God. Sin is seeking to become oneself, to get an identity, apart from him."[226]

- "God did not create us to get the cosmic, infinite joy of mutual love and glorification, but to share it. We are made to join in the dance."[227]

- "To know oneself, is above all, to know what one lacks. It is to measure oneself against the Truth, and not the other way around."[228]

- "If there is no God, then there is no way to say any one action is "more" and another "immoral" but only "I like this.""[229]

- "The resurrection of Jesus is a historical fact much more fully attested to than most other events of ancient history we take for granted."[230]

- "Jesus takes sides in debates that were going on in the early church."[231]

- "The Trinity means that God is, in essence, relational."[232]

- "...the empty tomb and the accounts of personal meetings with Jesus...must be taken together... No one in Jerusalem would have believed the preaching for a minute if the tomb was not empty... Paul could not be telling people in a public document that there were scores of eyewitnesses alive if there were not."[233]

- "For organic life to exist, the fundamental regularities and constants of physics – the speed of light, the gravitational constant, the strength of the weak and strong nuclear forces – must all have values that together fall into an extremely narrow

[226] Keller, 168.
[227] Keller, 228.
[228] Keller, 237.
[229] Keller, 159.
[230] Keller, 219.
[231] Keller, 108.
[232] Keller, 223.
[233] Keller, 212–13.

BOOKS TO READ

range. The probability of this perfect calibration happening by chance is so tiny as to be statistically negligible."[234]

Book Summary[235]:

Timothy Keller, the founding pastor of Redeemer Presbyterian Church in New York City, addresses the frequent doubts that skeptics, and even ardent believers, have about religion. Using literature, philosophy, real-life conversations, and potent reasoning, Keller explains how the belief in a Christian God is, in fact, a sound and rational one. To true believers he offers a solid platform on which to stand their ground against the backlash to religion created by the Age of Skepticism. And to skeptics, atheists, and agnostics, he provides a challenging argument for pursuing the reason for God.

Purchase Tips:

Always tried to buy used! *Always.*

Author Profile[236]:

Timothy Keller is senior pastor at Redeemer Presbyterian Church, Manhattan. He is renowned for his clear, reasoned approach to Christian apologetics and his book THE REASON FOR GOD: BELIEF IN AN AGE OF SKEPTICISM was named Book of the Year for 2008 by World Magazine.

---

[234] Keller, 134.
[235] All book summaries are cut and pasted from Amazon's website, however each one is the specific book summary put out by each book's publisher.
[236] This profile is the author's official biography available on Amazon.

BOOKS TO READ

"We are looking for that point of intersection where we think we are most likely to encounter God."[237]

Steven Charleston: The Four Vision Quests of Jesus[238]

BOOK SNIP

Type:
This is a text to read.

Topic Focus:
This book is important because it involves a deeply spiritual individual who struggles with, and eventually succeeds (beautifully, IMO) in melding the two very important sacred aspects of his life.

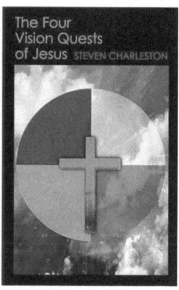

Sue's Thoughts;
Steven Charleston is a Native American Episcopal Bishop. The spiritual aspects of his Native American ancestry and the tenets of the Episcopal faith were difficult for him to unite and for a period of time it caused him great conflict. These two essential parts of him needed to be united and yet this seemed impossible. This book follows his journey in which he successfully accomplishes uniting his two faiths into one beautiful belief.

---

[237] Steven Charleston, *The Four Vision Quests of Jesus* (New York: Morehouse Publishing, 2015), 19. This is *another book* I read because of Dr. Virginia Wiles!
[238] Steven Charleston, *The Four Vision Quests of Jesus*.

90

This book was important for me for two reasons. First, it was fascinating to view the Gospel mission and message of Jesus through the eyes of another culture. Despite tremendously different perspectives, I still felt a solid unity with this new view. This book made me realize how Jesus Christ's life and message can fit in *anywhere* and perhaps more beautifully than my white, western version.

Second, Charleston speaks of a concept called a *thin place*. A *thin place* is not a geographic location but (my word) a dimension humanity can encounter where you feel there is an opportunity to best encounter God. It is that moment when you know you feel God's presence so profoundly that you get goosebumps and suddenly you and your existence is completely transformed. In actuality, many of these books that I have included in this book have given me *thin place* opportunities. And I want you to have them, too.

Favorite Quote(s):

- "The quest...is an act of placing ourselves in grace's way... These locations, which we sometimes call the thin places of reality, are not defined by geography, but by intention."[239]
- "The key to the seekers quest is not in finding just the right piece of holy real estate on which to stand, but rather in so preparing his or her awareness that any space he or she occupies can become thin through faith."[240]
- "When we place ourselves in the path of grace, when we open our minds and hearts to receive the presence of God, we are in the thin place of transformation."[241]
- "The quest becomes tangible because it becomes embodied. It is not a flight of the mind to imagine transcendence, but a

---

[239] Steven Charleston, 19.
[240] Steven Charleston, 19.
[241] Steven Charleston, 20.

BOOKS TO READ

movement of the very substance of human life to the place of meeting we can only describe as incarnation."[242]

- "The human quest is the risk of intimacy with God. It is going out to attempt to discover God and enter in communion with God."[243]

Book Summary[244]:

A unique look at Christian biblical interpretation and theology from the perspective of Native American tradition.

This book focuses on four specific experiences of Jesus as portrayed in the synoptic gospels. It examines each story as a "vision quest," a universal spiritual phenomenon, but one of particular importance within North American indigenous communities.

Jesus' experience in the wilderness is the first quest. It speaks to a foundational Native American value: the need to enter into the "we" rather than the "I." The Transfiguration is the second quest, describing the Native theology of transcendent spirituality that impacts reality and shapes mission. Gethsemane is the third quest. It embodies the Native tradition of the holy men or women, who find their freedom through discipline and concerns for justice, compassion, and human dignity. Golgotha is the final quest. It represents the Native sacrament of sacrifice (e.g., the Sun Dance). The chapter on Golgotha is a discussion of kinship, balance, and harmony: all primary to Native tradition and integral to Christian thought.

Purchase Tips:

Always tried to buy used! *Always.*

---

[242] Steven Charleston, 20.
[243] Steven Charleston, 20.
[244] All book summaries are cut and pasted from Amazon's website, however each one is the specific book summary put out by each book's publisher.

BOOKS TO READ

Author Profile:

Steven Charleston is a citizen of the Choctaw Nation of Oklahoma. He comes from a family with a long history of service in the Native American community. Ordained at Wakpala, South Dakota, on the Standing Rock Reservation, he has served as the national director for Native American ministries in the Episcopal Church, tenured professor of Systematic Theology at Luther Seminary, the bishop of Alaska, and president and dean of the Episcopal Divinity School in Cambridge, Massachusetts. Currently he teaches at the Saint Paul School of Theology at Oklahoma City University.[245]

---

[245] Steven Charleston, *The Four Vision Quests of Jesus*. This is from the back cover of the book.

"Your identity is in eternity, and your homeland is heaven."[246]

Rick Warren: The Purpose Driven Life[247]

BOOK SNIP

Type:
This is a text to be read.

Topic Focus:
This self-help book focuses on the meaning and purpose of your life and how to find God's perfect plan for it.

Sue's Thoughts;
After Oswald Chambers, this is the first Christian book that I read as an adult. A friend gave it to me as a gift[248] and I felt compelled to read it as a result. It was another one that made me a different person as a result.

Many of Warren's pithy statements have become my go to ones, like "The smile of God is the goal of your life."[249] An easy read, this book is perfect for new and "seasoned" believers providing valuable advice, insight, and opportunities for discussion.

If you are new to all this "Christian" reading stuff, this book would be a perfect place to start.

---

[246] Rick Warren, *The Purpose Driven Life* (Grand Rapids, Mich.: Zondervan Publishing House, 2002), 48.
[247] Warren, *The Purpose Driven Life*.
[248] Hi, Melanie!!!
[249] Warren, 88.

BOOKS TO READ

Favorite Quote(s):

- "God doesn't expect you to be perfect, but he does insist on complete honesty."[250]

- "Great opportunities may come once a in a lifetime, but small opportunities surround us every day."[251]

- "Did you know that admitting your hopelessness to God can be a statement of faith?"[252]

- "Never doubt in the dark what God told you in the light."[253]

- "The best use of life is love. The best expression of love is time. The best time to love is now."[254]

- "In resolving conflict, how you say it is as important as what you say."[255]

- "Your character is essentially the sum of your habits."[256]

- "God is far more interested in what you are than in what you do."[257]

- "Spiritual maturity is neither instant nor automatic; it is a gradual, progressive development that will take the rest of your life."[258]

- "The truth is, whatever you can't talk about is already out of control in your life."[259]

- "God never wastes anything."[260]

- "What I am able to do, God wants me to do."[261]

---

[250] Warren, 93.
[251] Warren, 96.
[252] Warren, 110.
[253] Warren, 111.
[254] Warren, 128.
[255] Warren, 157.
[256] Warren, 175.
[257] Warren, 177.
[258] Warren, 176.
[259] Warren, 213.
[260] Warren, 235.
[261] Warren, 243.

BOOKS TO READ

- "When God's at the center of your life, you worship. When he's not, you worry."[262]

Book Summary[263]:

Another Landmark Book by Rick Warren. You are not an accident. Even before the universe was created, God had you in mind, and he planned you for his purposes. These purposes will extend far beyond the few years you will spend on earth. You were made to last forever! Self-help books often suggest that you try to discover the meaning and purpose of your life by looking within yourself, but Rick Warren says that is the wrong place to start. You must begin with God, your Creator, and his reasons for creating you. You were made by God and for God, and until you understand that, life will never make sense. This book will help you understand why you are alive and God's amazing plan for you---both here and now, and for eternity. Rick Warren will guide you through a personal 40-day spiritual journey that will transform your answer to life's most important question: What on earth am I here for? Knowing God's purpose for creating you will reduce your stress, focus your energy, simplify your decisions, give meaning to your life, and, most importantly, prepare you for eternity. The Purpose Driven Life is a blueprint for Christian living in the 21st century---a lifestyle based on God's eternal purposes, not cultural values. Using over 1,200 scriptural quotes and references, it challenges the conventional definitions of worship, fellowship, discipleship, ministry, and evangelism. In the tradition of Oswald Chambers, Rick Warren offers distilled wisdom on the essence of what life is all about. This is a book of hope and challenge that you will read and re-read, and it will be a classic treasured by generations to come.

---

[262] Warren, 314.

[263] All book summaries are cut and pasted from Amazon's website, however each one is the specific book summary put out by each book's publisher.

BOOKS TO READ

Purchase Tips:

Always tried to buy used! *Always.*

Author Profile[264]:

Rick Warren is often called "America's most influential spiritual leader." He and his wife, Kay, founded Saddleback Church in Orange County, California, which is now one of the largest and best-known churches in the world. He also wrote the #1 all-time bestselling hardcover book, The Purpose Driven Life.

---

[264] This profile is the author's official biography available on Amazon.

"The object of the Christians' faith is unseen reality."[265]

A.W. Tozer: The Pursuit of God[266]

BOOK SNIP

Type:
This is a text to read.

Topic Focus:
Tozer focuses on the ways in which humanity must choose to live and act in order to have a life of true faith.

Sue's Thoughts;
Tozer has been around for a long time, born in 1897.[267] Over his life he would

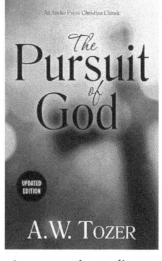

be influential in multiple Christian mediums (pastor, author, editor, mentor) and besides the twelve books he would eventually publish something like forty other books have been put together using his magazine articles, editorials, and sermons.

Tozer supposedly wrote this short little book on a train ride. While not long in length it is very deep causing readers to really think about themselves and their relationship with God. You can't read it quickly; you sort of have to "eat" it in small bites – but what a meal!

---

[265] A.W. Tozer, *The Pursuit of God: The Human Thirst for the Divine* (Camp Hill, PA: Christian Publications, n.d.), 54.
[266] Tozer, *The Pursuit of God: The Human Thirst for the Divine.*
[267] And died in 1963.

BOOKS TO READ

I've read other books by Tozer – "Meditations on the Trinity"[268] and "On the Holy Spirit"[269] to name a few. All are good and all have been transformational for me.

Favorite Quote(s):

- "…if my fire is not large it is yet real, and there may be those who can light their candle at its flame."[270]

- *"God is always previous*…. God's previous working meets man's present response."[271]

- "Our Lord came not to destroy but to save. Everything is safe which we commit to Him, and nothing is really safe which is not so committed."[272]

- "A spiritual kingdom lies all about us, enclosing us, embracing us, altogether within reach of our inner selves, waiting for us to recognize it."[273]

- "God has objective existence independent of and apart from any notions which we may have concerning Him. The worshiping heart does not create its Object."[274]

- "We habitually think of the visible world as real and doubt the reality of any other."[275]

- "We must shift our interest from the seen to the unseen. For the great unseen Reality is God…If we truly want to follow God, we must seek to be other-worldly."[276]

- "…*faith is the gaze of a soul upon a saving God.*"[277]

---

[268] A.W. Tozer, *Meditations on the Trinity* (Chicago, IL: Moody Publishers, n.d.).
[269] A.W. Tozer, *Tozer on the Holy Spirit* (Chicago: Moody Publishers, n.d.).
[270] Tozer, *The Pursuit of God: The Human Thirst for the Divine*, 10.
[271] Tozer, 12.
[272] Tozer, 28.
[273] Tozer, 50.
[274] Tozer, 53.
[275] Tozer, 53.
[276] Tozer, 54.
[277] Tozer, 83.

BOOKS TO READ

- "…faith is not a once-done act, but a continuous gaze of the heart at the Triune God. Believing, then, is directing the heart's attention to Jesus."[278]
- "Let us believe that God is in all our simple deeds and learn to find him there."[279]
- "Let every man abide in the calling wherein he is called and his work will be as sacred as the work of the ministry. It is not what a man does that determines whether his work is sacred or secular, it is why he does it. The motive is everything. Let a man sanctify the Lord God in his heart and he can thereafter do no common act."[280]

Book Summary[281]:

To have found God and still to pursue Him is a paradox of love, scorned indeed by the too-easily-satisfied religious person, but justified in happy experience by the children of the burning heart. Saint Bernard of Clairvaux stated this holy paradox in a musical four-line poem that will be instantly understood by every worshipping soul:

We taste Thee, O Thou Living Bread,
And long to feast upon Thee still:
We drink of Thee, the Fountainhead
And thirst our souls from Thee to fill.

Come near to the holy men and women of the past and you will soon feel the heat of their desire after God. Let A. W. Tozer's pursuit of God spur you also into a genuine hunger and thirst to truly know God.

---

[278] Tozer, 84.
[279] Tozer, 117.
[280] Tozer, 121.
[281] All book summaries are cut and pasted from Amazon's website, however each one is the specific book summary put out by each book's publisher.

BOOKS TO READ

Purchase Tips:

Always tried to buy used! *Always.*

Author Profile[282]:

A.W. TOZER (1897–1963) began his lifelong pursuit of God after hearing a street preacher in Akron, Ohio, at the age of seventeen. The self-taught theologian committed his life to the ministry of God's Word as a pastor, teacher, and writer. For his flowing prose, Spirit-filled words, and deep conviction, many have called him a modern-day prophet. He is the author of the beloved classic The Pursuit of God and dozens of other works.

---

[282] This profile is the author's official biography available on Amazon.

About The Author

Susan McGeown is a wife, mother, daughter, sister, friend, aunt, uncle (don't ask), teacher, author … but, most importantly, a "woman after God's own heart." Always working on a new book, she writes historical novels, contemporary fiction novels, and nonfiction Bible studies.

She's been a teacher, a conference leader, a public speaker, a children's minister, a deacon, an elder, a vacation Bible school coordinator, a preschool director, and a Bible study leader yet writing stories is just about the best way she can imagine spending her time. Lately, because she's not busy enough, she's become a seminary student.

Living in Bridgewater, New Jersey, with her husband of over thirty years, each of Sue's stories champions those emotions nearest and dearest to her: faith, joy, hope and love.

Philippians 1:20-21: *I earnestly expect and hope that I will in no way be ashamed but will have sufficient courage so that now, as always, Christ will be exalted in my life. For me, to live is Christ and to die is gain.*

Bibliography

Chambers, Oswald. *My Utmost for His Highest*. Uhrichsville, OH: Barbour Publishing, Inc., 1935.

Giles, Keith. *Jesus Unbound*. Orange, CA: Quoir, 2018.

Harrison, ed. *NLT Study Bible: New Living Translation*. Carol Stream, IL: Tyndale House Publishers, Inc., 2008.

Japinga, Lynn. *Feminism and Christianity: The Essential Guide*. Nashville, TN: Abingdon Press, 1999.

John, Jeffrey. *The Meaning in the Miracles*. Grand Rapids, Mich.: William B. Eerdmans Publishing Company, 2001.

Keller, Tim. *The Reason for God*. New York: Riverhead Books, 2008.

LeClaire, Jennifer. *Evenings With the Holy Spirit: Listening Daily to the Still, Small Voice of God*. Charisma House, 2024.

———. *Mornings With The Holy Spirit*. Lake Mary, FL: Charisma House, n.d.

Lewis, C. S. *Mere Christianity*. Revised Enlarged edition. San Francisco: HarperOne, 2023.

McGeown, Susan Lee. *C.S. Lewis & Me: Mere Christianity In Pictures*. CreateSpace Independent Publishing Platform, 2013.

McLaren, Brian D. *We Make the Road by Walking: A Year Long Quest for Spiritual Formation, Reorientation, and Activation*. New York: Jericho Books, 2015.

Pavlovitz, John. *If God Is Love Don't Be A Jerk: Finding a Faith That Makes Us Better Humans*. Louisville, KY: Westminster John Knox Press, 2021.

Peterson, Eugene H. *The Message: The Bible In Contemporary Language*. NavPress, 2006.

Rohr, Richard. *The Universal Christ*. New York: Covergent Books, n.d.

———. *Yes, And...* Cincinnati, OH: Franciscan Media, 1997.

Ruden, Sarah. *Paul Among the People*. New York: Image Books, 2010.

———. *The Gospels*. New York: Modern Library, 2021.

Spangler, Ann, and Jean E. Syswerda. *Women of the Bible: A One-Year Devotional Study of Women in Scripture*. Grand Rapids, Mich.: Zondervan Publishing House, 1999.

Stanley, Andy. *Irresistible - Reclaiming the New That Jesus Unleashed for the World*. Grand Rapids, Mich.: Zondervan Reflective, 2018.

Steven Charleston. *The Four Vision Quests of Jesus*. New York: Morehouse Publishing, 2015.

Thurman, Howard. *Jesus and the Disinherited*. Boston, MA: Beacon Press, 1976.

———. *Meditations of the Heart*. Boston, MA: Beacon Press, 1981.

Tozer, A.W. *Meditations on the Trinity*. Chicago, IL: Moody Publishers, n.d.

———. *The Pursuit of God: The Human Thirst for the Divine*. Camp Hill, PA: Christian Publications, n.d.

———. *Tozer on the Holy Spirit*. Chicago: Moody Publishers, n.d.

Warren, Rick. *The Purpose Driven Life*. Grand Rapids, Mich.: Zondervan Publishing House, 2002.

Wright, N. T. *Surprised by Hope: Rethinking Heaven, the Resurrection, and the Mission of the Church*. 1st ed. New York: HarperOne, 2008.

Yancey, Philip. *Prayer - Does It Make Any Difference*. Grand Rapids, Mich.: Zondervan Publishing House, 2006.